Toward Competition
in
Cable Television

AEI Studies in Telecommunications Deregulation

J. Gregory Sidak and Paul W. MacAvoy, series editors

TOWARD COMPETITION IN LOCAL TELEPHONY
William J. Baumol and J. Gregory Sidak

TOWARD COMPETITION IN CABLE TELEVISION
Leland L. Johnson

Toward Competition
in
Cable Television

Leland L. Johnson

THE MIT PRESS
Cambridge, Massachusetts
London, England

and

THE AMERICAN ENTERPRISE INSTITUTE
FOR PUBLIC POLICY RESEARCH
Washington, D.C.

Published by

The MIT Press
Cambridge, Massachusetts
London, England

and

The American Enterprise Institute for Public Policy Research
Washington, D.C.

Library of Congress Cataloging-in-Publication Data

Johnson, Leland L.
  Toward competition in cable television / Leland L. Johnson.
    p.   cm. — (AEI studies in telecommunications deregulation)
    Includes bibliographical references and indexes.
    ISBN 0-262-10054-1
    1. Cable Television—United States. 2. Competition—United
  States. I. Title. II. Series.
  HE8700.72.U6J64 1994
  384.55'51—dc20   94-15795
                                                            CIP

Printed in the United States of America

To Betty, Carl, and Steven

Contents

x

Foreword

DRAMATIC ADVANCES IN COMMUNICATIONS and information technologies are imposing severe strains on a government regulatory apparatus devised in the pioneer days of radio and are raising policy questions with large implications for American economic performance and social welfare. Is federal telecommunications regulation impeding competition and innovation, and has this indeed become its principal if unstated function? Is regulation inhibiting the dissemination of ideas and information through electronic media? Does the licensing regime for the electromagnetic spectrum allocate that resource to its most productive uses? If telecommunications regulation is producing any of these ill effects, what are the costs and offsetting benefits and what should be done?

Leland L. Johnson's study, presenting an effective framework for bringing competition to the cable television industry, is one of a series of research monographs addressing these questions commissioned by the American Enterprise Institute's Telecommunications Deregulation Project. The AEI project is intended to produce new empirical research on the entire range of telecommunications policy issues, with particular emphasis on identifying reforms to federal and state regulatory policies that will advance rather than inhibit innovation and consumer welfare. We hope this research will be useful to legislators and public officials at all levels of government, and to the business executives and, most of all, the consumers who must live with their policies. The monographs have been written and edited to be accessible to readers with no specialized knowledge of communications technologies or economics; we hope they will find a place in courses on regulated industries and communications policy in economics and communications departments and in business, law, and public policy schools.

Each monograph in the Telecommunications Deregulation Project has been discussed and criticized in draft form at an AEI seminar involving federal and state regulators, jurists, business executives, professionals, and academic experts with a wide range of interests and viewpoints, and has been reviewed and favorably reported by two anonymous academic referees selected by the MIT Press. I wish to thank all of them for their contributions, noting, however, that the final exposition and conclusions are entirely the responsibility of the author of each monograph.

I am particularly grateful to Dean Paul W. MacAvoy of the Yale School of Management and J. Gregory Sidak, resident scholar at AEI, for conceiving and overseeing the project's research and seminars, and to Frank Urbanowski, Terry Vaughn, and Ann Sochi of the MIT Press, for their support and steady counsel in seeing the research through to publication.

CHRISTOPHER C. DEMUTH
President, American Enterprise Institute
for Public Policy Research

Acknowledgments

THE IDEAS IN THIS MONOGRAPH were drawn from long discussions during recent years with Bridger M. Mitchell and David P. Reed. While they, and others below, will not agree with everything said, the study has benefited enormously from these longstanding collegial relationships. I owe a special debt of gratitude to J. Gregory Sidak, who provided extraordinarily helpful guidance and encouragement throughout the project. I am grateful, too, for the perceptive comments on the draft manuscript offered by Paul W. MacAvoy, Timothy J. Brennan, William Shew, and two anonymous referees selected by the MIT Press. Donald Dulchinos, Evan Kwerel, Jonathan Levy, Jack Linthicum, David Nicoll, Thomas Spavins, Peyton Wynns, and Larry Yokell were helpful in patiently answering my many questions and supplying data and other information throughout the course of the study. Many useful suggestions were offered by participants in a roundtable discussion of a draft of the study at the American Enterprise Institute in October 1993. I wish to thank Julie Bassett, who prepared the final manuscript for publication, with assistance from Douglas Ashton and Helgi Walker. Finally, I am forever indebted to Carol Richards who, with great patience and skill, keystroked countless revisions.

About the Author

LELAND L. JOHNSON, a consultant in telecommunications economics, retired in 1993 from RAND, Santa Monica, where he had been employed, with two interruptions for government service, since 1957. During 1978–79, he was Associate Administrator for Policy Analysis and Development in the National Telecommunications and Information Administration in Washington, D.C. In that capacity, Mr. Johnson was director of an office that, as adviser to the White House, focused on issues of reducing government regulation in the domestic telephone and broadcasting fields, expanding competitive pressures in the international communications industry, and making more effective use of the radio spectrum. During 1967–68, he was research director of the President's Task Force on Communications Policy in Washington. There the author directed the staff activities and preparation of the final report (the Rostow report) delivered to the President in 1968. The report and accompanying staff papers addressed a wide range of issues in the telephone, cable, and broadcasting fields, with numerous specific recommendations for national policy.

Mr. Johnson's subsequent studies at RAND spanned a wide range of telecommunications areas including the development of high-definition television, subsidies for telephone service to encourage universal coverage, development of technical compatibility standards, and international trade in telecommunications equipment. In recent years, he has focused on telephone company entry into video, including effects of advances in fiber optics and other technologies. Mr. Johnson has presented numerous seminars and briefings and has testified before congressional subcommittees and government administrative agencies.

He received his Ph.D. in economics from Yale University in 1957.

Toward Competition
in
Cable Television

1

Introduction

WE ARE WITNESSING an avalanche of new technologies aimed at providing a host of video services to the home; a growing list of companies that are, or want to be, players in this arena; and continuing controversy about government's proper role in response to today's virtual monopoly held by cable operators in wireline video delivery. Accordingly, numerous questions arise about sources of existing and future competition and the ingredients of well-conceived public policy to guide the creative energies of the players into the next century.

In response, this monograph is directed to two objectives. First, it seeks to identify the most likely sources of competition during the remainder of this decade. In light of possibilities for applying fiber-optic technologies to both telephone and video services, for example, what are the prospects for telephone companies to compete successfully against incumbent cable operators? What about direct broadcast satellites (DBS), whose development was marked by the launch of a high-power satellite in December 1993? What does the future hold for rapidly growing terrestrial wireless video systems? What role might be played by today's broadcasting stations if converted to offer advanced multichannel services? More generally, how soon is the cable television industry likely to face "effective" competition as defined in the Cable Television Consumer Protection and Competition Act of 1992? Technological and marketing uncertainties put any such prognostications on slippery ground. The one thing we can be certain about is a bundle of surprises.

Accordingly, the second, and more important, challenge of this monograph is to identify and assess ingredients of well-conceived public policy flexible enough to accommodate whatever technological and marketing opportunities, and disappointments, emerge. The objective is to provide inputs into a legislative and regulatory framework designed to ensure that firms with the lowest costs (for given outputs) are the ones most likely to survive, rather than those whose success stems either from their anticompetitive activities or from handicaps imposed on their competitors through misguided legislative and regulatory constraints.

Consistent with this purpose, the following questions are paramount. What would be the consequences of lifting the cross-ownership prohibition against telephone companies offering cable television in their local operating territories in competition with incumbent cable operators? Should telephone companies be required to offer their video channels under terms of nondiscriminatory access to all program suppliers? Do threats exist of cross-subsidy and other anticompetitive behavior, and what safeguards are appropriate? Are strategic alliances between telephone companies and cable operators likely to be procompetitive or anticompetitive? What are the consequences of some rivals being subject to municipal franchising and regulation, and others not, depending on the particular technologies employed?

Early Concerns About Monopoly Power

During the 1960s and 1970s, public policy debates were grounded on the presumption that cable television networks were natural monopolies. Into the foreseeable future, it was commonly argued, the home would be served by only one cable company for the same reason that it would be served by a single telephone system: construction of a competitive parallel network would entail wasteful duplication. The primary competitor to cable, over-the-air broadcasting, was sharply constrained by the limited radio spectrum. The abundance of channels offered by cable raised prospects of an exciting array of new services—but accessible only on a monopoly basis.

Consequently, much of the early policy debate focused on how to protect subscribers against monopoly pricing and to ensure adequate access by program providers to cable channels. The local franchise required by the cable operator for access to public rights of way was generally regarded as a key instrument of public control. Of paramount concern were questions of how franchise contracts should be written to best serve the public interest. Typically, policy recommendations involved combinations of price regulation and imposition of public service obligations (for example, "free" channels for use by schools and local governments) in exchange for the privileges enjoyed by cable franchisees.[1] At the same time, to leave open the possibility of competitive entry, it was commonly urged that franchise contracts be written on a nonexclusive basis.

Following such recommendations, most cable systems were subject to rate regulation by the cognizant local government agency, under terms stipulated in the franchise. This regulatory regime triggered criticism from the cable industry. Many companies complained of the cumbersome and time-consuming process of government approval for rate increases, which, among other things, discouraged network expansion and development of new programming. Moreover, competitive pressures, unforeseen in earlier decades, allegedly rendered government regulation increasingly unnecessary and inappropriate. Despite the growth of cable, the number of commercial and public television broadcasting stations grew from 953 to 1,505 from 1975 to 1992.[2] The home videocassette market enjoyed explosive growth, while direct broadcast satellite systems, planned during the early 1980s, posed a new competitive threat.

The Cable Communications Policy Act of 1984

In response to these competitive pressures and complaints by cable operators, Congress passed the Cable Communications Policy Act of

---

1. For major policy statements, see CABINET COMMITTEE ON COMMUNICATIONS, CABLE: REPORT TO THE PRESIDENT (1974); COMMITTEE FOR ECONOMIC DEVELOPMENT, BROADCASTING AND CABLE TELEVISION (1975); SLOAN COMMISSION ON CABLE COMMUNICATIONS, ON THE CABLE (McGraw-Hill 1971). A related debate focused on whether franchises should simply be auctioned to the highest bidder, with proceeds channeled to the public treasury. *See* Harold Demsetz, *Why Regulate Utilities?*, 11 J.L. & ECON. 55 (1968); Richard A. Posner, *The Appropriate Scope of Regulation in the CATV Industry*, 3 BELL J. ECON. 98 (1972); Oliver E. Williamson, *Franchise Bidding for Natural Monopolies—In General and With Respect to CATV*, 7 BELL J. ECON. 73 (1976).

2. TV AND CABLE FACTBOOK NO. 61, at C-17 (Warren Publishing Inc. 1993). Most of this growth was accounted for by UHF stations, which rose in number from 344 to 826, compared with a growth from 609 to 679 for VHF stations.

1984.[3] Among its provisions, the Cable Act permitted franchising authorities to regulate basic cable rates only in those cases where the cable system was not subject to "effective competition." The Act directed the Federal Communications Commission to define the circumstances under which effective competition existed and to review its regulations periodically, taking into account advances in technology.

Accordingly, the FCC decided in 1985 that a cable system was subject to effective competition if three or more unduplicated broadcasting signals were available within its service area.[4] Under this criterion, most cable systems qualified for rate deregulation, which became effective in November 1986.

Subsequently, cable rates rose rapidly. According to one study, four and a half years after deregulation (November 1986 to April 1991) the monthly rate for the lowest priced service had risen by 56 percent and for the most popular service by 61 percent—more than three times the rate of general inflation.[5] These increases, combined with numerous complaints of cable service deficiencies, generated widespread public pressure for "reregulation."

Demands for reregulation were met by the cable industry with claims that, during the same period, many more channels were made available, justifying the higher rates. At the same time, according to a recent econometric study, 43 percent of the total real price increase for basic service between the time the Cable Act was passed and the end of 1989 was due to the exercise of market power, not from improved service or other factors.[6]

In 1990, when demands for remedial measures were mounting, the FCC sent Congress a comprehensive report that drew from numerous filings by interested parties. The Commission concluded that cable

3. Pub. L. No. 98-549, 98 Stat. 2779 (codified as amended at 47 U.S.C. § 521).

4. Implementation of the Provisions of the Cable Communications Policy Act of 1984, Report and Order, MM Dkt. No. 84-1296, 50 Fed. Reg. 18,637 (1985).

5. HOUSE COMM. ON ENERGY AND COMMERCE, CABLE TELEVISION CONSUMER PROTECTION AND COMPETITION ACT OF 1992, H.R. REP. NO. 628, 102d Cong., 2d Sess. 33 (1992).

6. *See* Robert Rubinovitz, *Market Power and Price Increases for Basic Cable Service Since Deregulation*, 24 RAND J. ECON. 47 (1993).

systems "do possess varying degrees of market power in local distribution."[7] It rejected the notion of reregulation as a remedy, however, favoring instead the encouragement of competition:

> This Commission steadfastly believes that robust competition will more effectively provide both a better safeguard against undue rate increases or service failings and a greater diversity and choice than any web of rules and regulations designed to mimic competition or otherwise compensate for its absence.[8]

The Commission's reasoning left open a key question: if cable systems have varying degrees of market power, and if reregulation through legislation is to be avoided, how is the public to be protected from cable's market power? For the long term, the answer is easily enough couched in terms of promoting competition. In the short term, however, the answer is less obvious, since time and appropriate government policies are required for competitive alternatives to develop, even if economic and technical factors are favorable for competition. How is the public to be protected in the meantime?

The FCC responded by reassessing the ingredients of effective competition. If unregulated cable systems demonstrate market power while meeting the Commission's three-signal test, a stricter test might be appropriate—all the more so, since it could be adopted without revision of the 1984 Cable Act.

The Commission concluded that effective competition is deemed to exist if either

> (a) six unduplicated over-the-air broadcast television signals are available in the entire cable community, or (b) an independently owned, competing multichannel video delivery system is available to 50 percent of the homes passed by the incumbent cable system and subscribed to by at least 10 percent of the homes passed by the

---

7. Competition, Rate Deregulation, and the Commission's Policies Relating to the Provision of Cable Television Service, Report, MM Dkt. No. 89-600, 5 F.C.C. Rcd. 4962, 5003 ¶ 69 (1990) [hereinafter *1990 Cable Report*].

8. *Id.* at 4969 ¶ 8.

alternative system within the incumbent cable system's service area.[9]

The Cable Television Consumer Protection and Competition Act of 1992

Despite the Commission's pursuit of procompetitive policies and its stricter six-signal test for effective competition, pressure continued to mount for congressional action. Under the six-signal standard, the bulk of the nation's cable subscribers would remain dependent on unregulated service. Moreover, effective multichannel competition was yet to develop.[10] In the closing days of the 102d Congress, after extraordinarily heated debate and lobbying efforts, the Cable Television Consumer Protection and Competition Act of 1992 was enacted into law—over presidential veto.[11]

Because the definition of effective competition adopted in the 1992 Act is more stringent than the six-signal standard previously adopted by the Commission, few cable systems today are exempted from its provisions. Section 623 of the Act deems effective competition to exist under any of three circumstances:

1. Fewer than 30 percent of the households in the franchise area take cable service. This provision is based on the notion that competition, whether from broadcasters or from other sources, reduces the cable subscriber (penetration) rate. Thus, competition that is strong enough to force cable subscribership below 30 percent is regarded as

9. Reexamination of the Effective Competition Standard for the Regulation of Cable Television Basic Service Rates, Report and Order and Second Further Notice of Proposed Rulemaking, MM Dkt. Nos. 90-4, 84-1296, 6 F.C.C. Rcd. 4545, 4545 ¶ 1 (1991).

10. The General Accounting Office concluded that 59 percent of the cable systems servicing 80 percent of the nation's subscribers were not subject to regulation under the "six-signal" standard. GENERAL ACCOUNTING OFFICE, 1991 SURVEY OF CABLE TELEVISION RATES AND SERVICES 4 (1991).

11. Pub. L. No. 102-385, 106 Stat. 1460 (codified as amended at 47 U.S.C. § 533). *See* President's Message to the Senate Returning Without Approval the Cable Television Consumer Protection and Competition Act of 1992, 28 WEEKLY COMP. PRES. DOC. 1860 (Oct. 3, 1992). The veto was consistent with the Bush administration's advocacy of less regulation of telecommunications markets.

effective. This line of reasoning is troubling. The link between penetration and market power is not obvious. A penetration rate above 30 percent could result from superior performance in a highly competitive marketplace. Conversely, a low penetration rate might reflect a cable operator's decision to remain below the 30 percent threshold if the combination of lower penetration and unregulated subscriber rates yields greater profits than would higher penetration and regulated rates.[12]

2.   The franchise area is served by two or more unaffiliated multichannel video distributors, each offering comparable programming to at least 50 percent of the households, with at least 15 percent of the households subscribing to a service other than that of the largest distributor (presumably the incumbent cable operator). This provision is similar to the FCC's earlier specification for multichannel competition.   In a subsequent rulemaking, the Commission concluded that to offer comparable programming, multichannel video programmers "must provide at least twelve channels of programming, including at least one channel of nonbroadcast service programming."[13]   Observing that few cable systems offer fewer than twelve channels, the Commission decided that "this is the minimum number of channels which a competitor must offer to be found 'comparable' in programming to an incumbent cable operator."[14] The Commission further decided that only those multichannel programming distributors that offered programming to at least 50 percent of the households in the franchise area would be included in the cumulative measurement of market share.[15] Thus, for example, a 3 percent market share of a competitor to the incumbent cable

12. The FCC considered a penetration criterion in its investigation that led to its six-signal standard, but it rejected the approach for the reasons noted above. Report and Order, *supra* note 9, at 4551 ¶¶ 28-29.

13. Implementation of Sections of the Cable Television Consumer Protection and Competition Act of 1992: Rate Regulation, Report and Order and Further Notice of Proposed Rulemaking, MM Dkt. No. 92-266, 8 F.C.C. Rcd. 5631, 5666 ¶ 38 (1993) [hereinafter *Rate Regulation Order*].

14. *Id.* at 5665 ¶ 37.

15. *Id.* at 5663 ¶ 36.

system would not be included in the 15 percent minimum cumulative share if this service were available to only 40 percent of the households.

3. A competing provider, operated by the franchising authority itself (generally the municipality), offers service to at least 50 percent of the households within the franchise area (with no stipulation about actual sign-ups). This provision is based on the (questionable) premise that a publicly owned system is better able to serve the public interest than a privately owned one. Regardless of how few households subscribe to the publicly owned service, it is deemed to offer effective competition if it is available to at least 50 percent of the households.

The Act generally provides that where effective competition exists, cable television rates shall not be subject to government regulation.[16] In the absence of effective competition, regulation is to be undertaken jointly by the FCC and by state and local governments. For purposes of allocating regulatory responsibilities, the Act distinguishes among four categories of cable service.

The first category, the "basic-service tier," includes, at a minimum, the broadcast signals transmitted by the cable operator, along with any public, educational, and government (PEG) access channels that the local franchise authority requires the cable operator to carry on the basic tier. Regulation of rates for this category is generally the responsibility of state and local governments.

The second category, "cable-programming service," includes all video programming that is not on the basic-service tier and for which the operator does not charge on a per-channel or per-program basis. This category is subject to regulation by the Commission, but only in response to specific complaints about an operator's cable programming service.

The third category includes programming for which the cable operator does charge a per-channel or per-program fee. The rates for this

16. 47 U.S.C. § 543(a)(2).

category are not subject to regulation.

The fourth category is for "commercial leased access," which includes those channels required by the Act to be available for lease by outside unaffiliated parties. The terms and rates for these channels are subject to Commission regulation.

The 1992 Act includes several provisions designed to encourage competition, with the FCC directed to formulate specific rules:

- Franchising authorities are prohibited from writing exclusive franchises, and they are directed not to "unreasonably refuse" to award an additional franchise.

- Cable operators and their affiliated program suppliers are prohibited from engaging in practices that hinder or prevent other multichannel systems from competing.

- A uniform rate structure is mandated throughout a franchise area to forestall attempts by the cable operator to drive out a newcomer by selectively cutting rates within the geographical area of competition.

- Limitations are to be imposed on the number of cable subscribers that any one cable operator may reach nationwide and on the number of channels that may be used by vertically integrated programmers on a system owned by their cable affiliate.

- Cable operators are prohibited from owning either of two types of wireless multichannel systems that operate in their franchise areas: (1) multichannel, multipoint distribution service (MMDS) —commonly known by the oxymoron "wireless cable"—which uses a microwave frequency band for transmission of multiple video channels to subscribers from a local MMDS transmitter, and (2) satellite master antenna (SMATV) systems, which feed satellite signals from a master antenna to dwelling units within a building or cluster of buildings.

As mandated by the Act, the Commission established in April 1993 the framework for regulating the rates of cable systems.[17] It adopted a "benchmark" approach in which the basic-tier rates for cable systems are to be rolled back to the levels determined to exist for systems that are subject to effective competition. With other factors constant, the Commission's analysis showed a competitive differential of about 10 percent.[18] If systems in low penetration areas (below 30 percent) are excluded, however, the differential rises to about 28 percent.[19] After further consideration, the Commission concluded that the "clear statutory language" of the Act requires the Commission to include data from low-penetration systems in its calculations of ceilings for the regulation of cable rates.[20] Thus, the inclusion of low-penetration systems (which is a questionable criterion for determining the presence of effective competition) has reduced the degree to which government regulation will force rates to fall.

After the Commission's mandated rollback of regulated rates by an average of 10 percent, consumer complaints persisted about continuing rate increases, or insufficient decreases. In response, the Commission ordered in February 1994 an additional 7 percent rollback, amid complaints from cable operators that this action would seriously impede their plans for investment in advanced networks.[21]

System operators who believe that they can justify higher rates based on costs are free to seek exemptions based on cost-of-service studies. But this provision gives little basis for cheer among cable operators. The Commission's own words describe how they will face the same costly, time-consuming, and cumbersome regulatory procedures that have marked the history of the telephone industry:

---

17. *Rate Regulation Order, supra* note 13.

18. *Id.* at 5977 ¶ 560.

19. *Id.* at 5977 ¶ 561.

20. Implementation of Sections of the Cable Television Consumer Protection and Competition Act of 1992: Rate Regulation, First Order on Reconsideration, Second Report and Order, and Third Notice of Proposed Rulemaking, MM Dkt. No. 92-266, 9 F.C.C. Rcd. 1164, 1170 ¶ 6 (1993).

21. FCC Orders Further Rate Reduction While Preserving Incentives for Cable Operators to Invest in New Services (News Release, Feb. 22, 1994).

Cost of service proceedings may be elected by cable operators facing unusually high costs. Those operators will have their rates based on their allowable costs, in a proceeding based on principles similar to those that govern cost-based rate regulation of telephone companies. Under this methodology, cable operators may recover, through the rates they charge for regulated cable service, their normal operating expenses and a reasonable return on investment.[22]

Strategic Alliances

The plans announced during 1993 for mergers, joint ventures, and other strategic alliances between regional Bell operating companies (RBOCs) and cable multiple system operators (MSOs) have attracted a good deal of attention, especially with respect to how they may affect competition. In the most stunning announcement, Bell Atlantic, Tele-Communications Inc. (TCI), and Liberty Media announced plans to merge, a deal that subsequently collapsed in February 1994 in the wake of the Commission's decision to impose more stringent rate regulation on cable systems.[23] This move would have combined Bell Atlantic's assets with those of the nation's largest MSO. TCI, including its ties with Liberty, holds ownership interests with cable systems that pass 27 percent of the nation's homes.[24]

In other actions, Southwestern Bell has acquired the cable properties of Hauser Communications, in the Washington, D.C. area. These

---

22. Executive Summary, Implementation of Sections of the Cable Television Consumer Protection and Competition Act of 1992; Report and Order and Further Notice of Proposed Rulemaking, MM Docket No. 93-215 (Press Release, Feb. 22, 1994) at 1.

23. Bell Atlantic, *Bell Atlantic, TCI and Liberty Media to Merge*, Press Release, Oct. 13, 1993, at 2; *Bell Atlantic's Pact to Acquire TCI Collapses Amid Dispute Over Price; Cable Rate Cut Ordered by FCC Was Final Straw,* WALL ST. J., Feb. 24, 1994, at A3.

24. Implementation of Sections 11 and 13 of the Cable Television Consumer Protection and Competition Act of 1992, Horizontal and Vertical Ownership Limits, Second Report and Order, MM Dkt. No. 92-264, 8 F.C.C. Rcd. 3565, 8578 n.40 (1993).

systems pass 386,000 homes and serve 228,000 subscribers.[25] Moreover, Southwestern Bell had planned to commit $1.6 billion in a venture with Cox Cable Communications to enable the two entities to own and operate jointly twenty-one Cox cable systems with 1.62 million subscribers.[26] The deal collapsed, however, also after the Commission's decision to impose more stringent price regulation on cable systems.[27] U S West plans to invest $2.5 billion in Time Warner Entertainment, the nation's second largest MSO, with 7.1 million subscribers.[28] The transaction is designed to accelerate the development of two-way digital interactive television systems in Time Warner's cable franchise areas. Finally, BellSouth plans to acquire a 22.5 percent interest in Prime Management Co., a firm that manages five cable systems serving more than 500,000 subscribers.[29]

Despite the failed Bell Atlantic-TCI and Southwestern Bell-Cox plans, we must expect more alliances—RBOCs and independent telephone companies involved with out-of-territory cable systems, as well as with movie studios and other program suppliers.

Some Definitions

As illustrated by such alliances, some telephone companies outside their territories may become cable operators, while others in partnership with cable companies may compete within their territories with incumbent cable operators. To avoid confusion in this world of musical chairs, we need definitions of some terms that vary from common usage. Telephone companies that operate in local areas—local access and transport areas (LATAs)—are called local exchange carriers (LECs). These consist predominantly of the seven regional Bell operat-

25. Southwestern Bell Corp., *Southwestern Bell Corporation, Cox Cable Communications Sign Agreement to Form U.S. Cable Television Partnership*, Press Release, Dec. 7, 1993, at 6.

26. *Id.*

27. Anita Sharpe & Mark Robichaux, *Southwestern Bell and Cox Cancel Venture*, WALL ST. J., Apr. 6, 1994, at A3.

28. Time Warner, Inc., *Time Warner Entertainment and US West Close Strategic Partnership Investment*, Press Release, Sept. 15, 1993.

29. TELECOMMUNICATIONS REP., Oct. 18, 1993, at 10.

ing companies, which control about 80 percent of the nation's telephone access lines. The remaining 20 percent are held by independent telephone companies such as GTE and United Telecom (now known as Sprint). Recall that under the Modification of Final Judgment (MFJ), entered in 1982, the RBOCs were separated from AT&T, which is one of the "interexchange" carriers that compete in the long-distance (predominantly interLATA) market.[30]

In contrast, we confine the use of the term "LEC" to the local exchange carriers such as the Bell operating companies (BOCs)[31] that, in their own territories, are limited to offering only "video dialtone" in competing with incumbent cable operators. These LECs have parent companies, such as RBOCs in the case of the BOCs, that are free to acquire or otherwise to hold interests in cable systems outside the operating territories of their LECs. We generally refer to these parent telephone companies as local telephone companies, but in some cases, we use the term generically to include both parents and LECs, as in the chapter titles.

New Jersey Bell, for example, is a LEC that proposes to offer video dialtone in that state, while its parent, Bell Atlantic, might hold interests in out-of-territory cable systems (which, until the merger plan with TCI collapsed, would have been TCI properties). Thus, TCI properties to have been acquired by Bell Atlantic in California would have competed against whatever video offerings Pacific Bell (as a LEC) developed. In this way, Bell Atlantic, as an (out-of-territory) cable incumbent, might also offer local telephone service in competition with LECs. Thus, in our parlance, RBOCs and indepen-

---

30. United States *v.* American Tel. & Tel. Co., 552 F. Supp. 131 (D.D.C. 1982), *aff'd sub nom.*, Maryland *v.* United States, 460 U.S. 1001 (1983). For an exhaustive analysis of the MFJ and its subsequent interpretation, see MICHAEL K. KELLOGG, JOHN THORNE & PETER W. HUBER, FEDERAL TELECOMMUNICATIONS LAW (Little, Brown & Co. 1992).

31. A BOC is any one of the 22 telephone companies that were wholly owned by AT&T immediately before the divestiture, as well as "any entity directly or indirectly owned or controlled by a BOC or affiliated through substantial common ownership." *See* Modification of Final Judgment, United States *v.* American Tel. & Tel. Co., 552 F. Supp. at 228. Thus, among the affiliations, the definition of BOC includes their parent RBOCs.

dent local telephone companies (such as GTE) may compete with the LECs of other local telephone companies for video service and perhaps telephone service as well.

Further, we take "telephone" service as synonymous with "narrowband" service, which encompasses voice and data transmission generally up to speeds of 64,000 bits per second (64 Kbps). We take "video" service as synonymous with "television" service, which, in the absence of signal compression discussed in Chapter 3, requires "broadband" capacity. With speeds of 45 Mbps (forty-five million bits per second) or greater, a broadband channel suitable for television can carry many hundreds of telephone conversations.

Organization and Key Conclusions

Chapter 2 treats briefly the prospects for competitive entry by new cable operators (other than telephone companies) through construction of parallel networks in the territories of incumbents. Municipal governments and publicly owned electric utilities are among the participants in "overbuilding" existing cable systems. Economic constraints combined with possible local franchising problems, however, cloud the prospects for significant growth of overbuilding.

By far the largest portion of the study, encompassing three chapters, deals with the LECs. Chapter 3 treats the prospects for the LECs, using fiber-optic networks for both video and telephone service, to compete with incumbent cable systems (which may include systems owned by out-of-territory RBOCs or independent telephone companies). We assume that the LECs have the same freedom of action as do cable operators; that is, the two groups are on regulatory parity. We do so to facilitate assessment of how basic economic and technological factors are likely to affect outcomes. Despite the widespread interest in the use of fiber optics, we conclude that the LECs, at least during this decade, will have a tough time competing with cable systems, which are already accessible to more than 95 percent of the nation's homes. The prospects would be brighter if the LECs find a way to use their existing copper networks for satisfactory delivery of video.

Chapter 4 focuses on the prospects for the LECs to compete, given that they are today constrained to offer video only under common-carrier "video dialtone" rules established by the Commission. Under these rules, the LEC is not permitted to hold significant ownership interests in programming, and it must offer its channels on a nondiscriminatory basis to all prospective program suppliers. The rules were established because of concerns that otherwise the LECs would cross-subsidize their video activities from telephone revenues and that they would use their network bottlenecks anticompetitively against outside program suppliers. We conclude that the LECs will have even greater difficulty competing under these rules against cable operators, who are free of these burdens. We further conclude that video dialtone may prove nonviable in the face of regulatory asymmetry between the LECs and cable operators. Failure to achieve common-carrier status for video, however, may not pose a serious loss for society because the expansion of channel capacity will produce greater program diversity, with or without common carriage. Moreover, competition from other multichannel providers, such as DBS systems, will further encourage diversity, even if none operates as a common carrier.

Chapter 5 examines the potential consequences of lifting the cross-ownership ban to permit the LECs to engage in programming directly. We conclude that the ban should be lifted if for no other reason than that the ban has little to do with the commonly expressed fears that the LECs would engage in anticompetitive activities. The source of cross-subsidy arises from the integration of telephone and video services on the same transmission network, *not* from LEC ownership or control of programming. Moreover, concerns about possible anticompetitive use by LECs of their bottleneck network facilities can best be met by limitations on *horizontal* concentration—that is, the percentage of the nation's subscribers that can be served by a single multichannel operator. The limits already established by the Commission for cable operators could be carried over to the LECs if necessary. If safeguards against cross-subsidy are deemed adequate for common-carrier–based LEC video dialtone services, and if adequate limitations on horizontal concentration are in place, it inescapably follows that the cross-ownership ban should be lifted and the LECs granted full regulatory parity to compete with cable operators.

Chapter 6 treats the economic and technical characteristics of satellite-based systems as a substitute for wireline video distribution systems. By virtue of their nationwide coverage, direct broadcast satellites are strong potential competitors with cable systems. Outcomes will critically depend on how rapidly retail prices fall for home satellite receiving equipment.

Chapter 7 examines terrestrial wireless techniques for multichannel video transmission. These include wireless cable operating in the 2 GHz (two billion Hertz or cycles per second) microwave range, the emergence of local multichannel distribution systems (LMDS) operating in the 28 GHz range, and possibilities for today's local broadcasters to convert to multichannel operation by adopting digital signal-compression techniques. Wireless cable (like DBS systems) is also a strong near-term candidate for competition with cable. Outcomes will depend on how quickly wireless operators adapt signal-compression techniques to boost their channel capacities.

Moving beyond economic and technical analysis of individual types of video distribution systems, Chapter 8 deals with several key issues of public policy that cut across technologies. We conclude, among other things, that Congress erred in defining effective competition in terms of market shares alone. By the end of the decade, the combined subscribership to DBS and wireless cable systems, along with other multichannel alternatives to cable, will probably not reach the minimum level stipulated by the 1992 Cable Act as a condition for effective competition. Nevertheless, cable will face much competitive pressure. This situation will be difficult for cable operators because, even though facing competition, their rates will be subject to regulation until effective competition as defined in the Act is achieved.

Chapter 9 brings together major conclusions in the form of recommendations for action by Congress, the Commission, and state and local governments. We end optimistically by concluding that the path of well-conceived policy making among the contending parties is tolerably clear cut, with the American public standing to be the winner.

2

Competitive Cable Systems

THIS IS THE FIRST of four chapters devoted to the potential use of new wireline networks in competition with those of incumbent cable operators. This chapter is concerned with newcomers other than the LECs. These consist largely of privately owned cable systems and systems owned by municipalities, commonly in association with local publicly owned electric utilities. These networks, constructed in parallel with existing ones, are called second cable systems or overbuilds. Chapters 3, 4, and 5 treat the possibilities for LECs—a topic that has attracted the bulk of attention by industry groups, consumer advocates, and government policy makers in the multichannel video arena.

A Source of Limited Competition

Although we do not have complete data on the number of households with a choice between two competing cable systems, the number is not large. According to a 1992 census of overbuilding, some 1.3 million households were in communities with overlapping cable systems, only about 1.5 percent of the nation's homes passed by cable.[1] Moreover, the subset of households passed by multiple cable systems is even

---

1. Paul Kagan Associates, *Cable TV Overbuild Census*, CABLE TV FRANCHISING DATA ROUNDUP, Apr. 30, 1992. Specific cases of overbuilding are discussed by Thomas W. Hazlett, *Duopolistic Competition in Cable Television: Implications for Public Policy*, 7 YALE J. ON REG. 65 (1990).

smaller because these data include both duplicate cable coverage and situations where franchisees operate alone in adjacent service areas. Another survey disclosed that in 1991 overbuilding existed in only fifty-three communities out of some 11,000 cable franchises.[2]

To be sure, a few geographical areas exhibit substantial amounts of overbuilding. In Allentown, Pennsylvania, two cable operators exist side by side, encouraged by poor over-the-air reception caused by hilly terrain and high population diversity that reduces the per household cost of wireline construction. In Anne Arundel County, Maryland, a cable operator had obtained a franchise in 1973 but had built only fifteen miles of plant by the time a second entered in 1988. Subsequently, a "building frenzy" occurred, leaving some tens of thousands of homes in an overbuilt portion of the county.[3]

Occasionally, plans are announced for new overbuilding, presumably as a reflection of specific local conditions that improve the prospects for financial success. A notable example is the proposal announced in mid-1993 by the FiberVision Corporation to construct a cable system to serve Hartford, Connecticut, and surrounding communities.[4] The plan, approved in early 1994 by the Connecticut Department of Public Utility Control, calls for service to 65,000 homes with 300 miles of fiber-intensive cable plant.[5] Investment costs will be relatively low because of high population diversity (180 homes per mile of cable plant compared with a nationwide average of about 70 homes) and the use of aerial rather than more expensive underground installa-

---

2. SENATE COMM. ON COMMERCE, SCIENCE, AND TRANSPORTATION, CABLE TELEVISION CONSUMER PROTECTION ACT OF 1991, S. REP. NO. 92, 102d Cong., 1st Sess. 13 (1991) [hereinafter SENATE COMMITTEE REPORT].

3. Telephone interview with Chauncey Berdan, Cable Television Administrator, Anne Arundel County (Nov. 4, 1993). We cannot determine the precise number of homes with access to the two competing systems, because both do not pass all the homes in the overbuilt area. One system was reported in late 1993 to pass 38,060 homes; the other 22,000 homes. If all homes had access to both systems, the systems would report the same number of homes passed within the overbuilt area.

4. The FiberVision Corp., Press Release, July 8, 1993.

5. *Id.* at 2. Connecticut Department of Utility Control, Dkt. No. 93-07-04, Feb. 16, 1994.

tion.[6] FiberVision has also filed an application to serve the metropolitan areas of New Haven, Bridgeport, and New Britain.[7]

Economic Constraints

The paucity of overbuilding stems from its unfavorable economics. Suppose that an incumbent has paid $2,500 per subscriber for a recently acquired cable system with a plant replacement cost of $700 per subscriber—a common situation in the industry.[8] Suppose further that in the absence of competition, revenues are enough to justify the high purchase price. A prospective wireline entrant is attracted by the difference between the $2,500 per subscriber buying price and the $700 replacement cost, which suggests that substantial profits could be earned by constructing a similar plant alongside that of the incumbent, rather than by buying out the incumbent at a price of at least $2,500 per subscriber.

The incumbent, aware of this possibility, could reduce subscriber rates, however, if the newcomer threatens to initiate construction. At the financial limit, it could cut rates to its out-of-pocket or variable cost (that is, operating and other recurring expenses). To be sure, the incumbent might bankrupt itself in carrying out this strategy, since it could not recover the $2,500 purchase price. Nevertheless, the system would continue to be operated, either by the financially reorganized incumbent or by a new purchaser, as long as variable costs are covered. Only years later—when the network itself needs replacement—would the incumbent system be abandoned.

Further, wiring the area would require a large investment by the newcomer regardless of how many subscribers sign up. If the incumbent were to carry out its price-cutting strategy, the entrant

6. Telephone Interview with Donald Ryan, President, The FiberVision Corp. (Oct. 21, 1993).

7. The FiberVision Corp., Press Release, Oct. 5, 1993.

8. These assumed figures are in line with those estimated in Competition, Rate Deregulation, and the Commission's Policies Relating to the Provision of Cable Television Service, Report, MM Dkt. No. 89-600, 5 F.C.C. Rcd. 4962, 5076 n.11 (1990) [hereinafter *1990 Cable Report*].

would have little hope of recovering its cost for assets that are essentially nonsalvageable. Thus, the prospective wireline company would likely be deterred from entering, and the incumbent would be relieved of the need to reduce prices. This situation is an example of a "noncontestable" market.[9] In most cases, the incumbent is protected because the prospective newcomer faces costs of entry and exit that are too high to render the threat of entry credible. For this reason, threats of overbuilding typically are empty or lead to a buyout.[10] According to one source, mergers have occurred between the two existing or proposed systems in 62 of the 132 communities in which second franchises have been advanced or are under study.[11]

Many cases have arisen where incumbents have cut subscriber rates in the face of threatened or actual competition. As one example,

By the time the city of Glasgow, Kentucky had strung its first thousand feet of cable, its private competitor had dropped cable TV rates almost 60 percent, but only to that portion of the community that was wired for the city-owned system. As the municipally owned system's service territory grew, so did the area receiving the cut rates from the private operator. Now, subscribers of the private system who live one block outside of city limits are paying $4 more per month than customers of the same system who live in Glasgow.[12]

9. The seminal development of the concept of contestability is by WILLIAM J. BAUMOL, JOHN C. PANZAR & ROBERT D. WILLIG, CONTESTABLE MARKETS AND THE THEORY OF INDUSTRY STRUCTURE (Harcourt Brace Jovanovich, rev. ed. 1988). For a critical assessment of the concept, see William G. Shepherd, *Contestability vs. Competition*, 73 AM. ECON. REV. 572 (1984).

10. MULTICHANNEL NEWS, Apr. 13, 1987, at 17. For an informative example of the pressures to merge, in this case the sale of cable systems owned by Telesat Cablevision to a competitor, and the withdrawal of its applications for service in two Florida counties, see *Telesat Sells Out to Palmer in Two Florida Counties*, MULTICHANNEL NEWS, Aug. 14, 1989, at 22.

11. SENATE COMMITTEE REPORT, *supra* note 2, at 13.

12. Ted Coombes, *A New Law Could Spawn Creation of Many New Municipally-Owned Cable Communications Systems*, PUBLIC POWER, Jan.-Feb. 1993, at 15. For other examples, see Ann Dukes, *Telesat Set to Overbuild Televents in FL*, MULTICHANNEL NEWS, Mar. 14, 1988, at 36; Debbie Narrod, *Overbuilders Get Serious*, CABLE WORLD,

Such discriminatory practices were responsible for the provision in the 1992 Cable Act that requires the cable operator to have a rate structure "that is uniform throughout the geographic area in which cable service is provided over its cable system."[13]

More generally, rates in competitive markets are lower than those served by only a single cable operator. As noted in Chapter 1, the Commission found per-channel rates in competitive markets to be about 28 percent below those elsewhere.[14]

Local Franchise Barriers

Although perhaps less important today than in earlier years, the local franchising requirement has posed an entry barrier to overbuilders. It is commonly asserted that municipalities prefer an exclusive franchise arrangement because it permits them, in effect, to share in the monopoly profits of cable operators through the collection of fees and the imposition of other obligations specified in the franchise contract. Thomas W. Hazlett, for example, concludes that "the difficulties faced by competitive entrants arise not so much from natural monopoly conditions as from the ability of incumbent suppliers to transfer monopoly rents to municipal officials so as to protect their exclusive franchise."[15] In response, Albert K. Smiley argues that

Hazlett's assertion that municipalities routinely seek to impede competitive entry is supported by anecdotal evidence involving several overbuilds in Florida and Sacramento. However, in an industry with over 7,000 cable systems, and given the idiosyncrasies of local regulators and maverick operators, it is possible to find anecdotes to support almost any proposition. Thus, anecdotes tell us little about how franchising authorities generally

Mar. 5, 1990, at 22.

13. 47 U.S.C. § 543(d).

14. Implementation of Sections of the Cable Television Consumer Protection and Competition Act of 1992, Rate Regulation, MM Dkt. No. 92-266, 8 F.C.C. Rcd. 5631, 5977 ¶ 561 (1993).

15. Hazlett, *supra* note 1, at 66.

behave.[16]

Despite the presence of only anecdotal evidence of anticompetitive behavior, Congress included in the 1992 Cable Act provisions to ban exclusive franchises and to direct franchising authorities not to "unreasonably refuse" to award an additional franchise.[17] Even before the Act, however, most franchise contracts were written on a nonexclusive basis. The difficulty lies not in *de jure* exclusion but in the interpretation of what is and is not "unreasonable." Conditions established by the 1992 Act as not unreasonable are much the same as those used in the past to discourage competitive cable entry. The Act, for example, stipulates that the franchising authority may require "adequate assurance" that the new applicant has the financial, technical, and legal qualifications to provide service[18] and will provide "adequate" PEG channel capacity, facilities, and financial support.[19]

Aside from this congressional initiative, municipalities are under greater pressure today than in earlier years to promote competition because of public complaints about cable rate hikes and poor service.[20] One manifestation is interest by some municipalities in building systems in competition with privately owned incumbents.

Entry by Municipalities and Electric Utilities

Some municipalities and publicly owned electric utilities are active in existing and contemplated overbuilds of privately owned systems. According to a survey in early 1993, sixty-two cable systems are municipally owned, of which thirty-nine are associated with the municipally owned electric power system.[21] Altogether, the sixty-two

16. Albert K. Smiley, *Regulation and Competition in Cable Television*, 7 YALE J. ON REG. 121, 124-25 (1990).

17. 47 U.S.C. § 541.

18. *Id.* § 541(a)(4)(C).

19. *Id.* § 541(a)(4)(B).

20. WARREN'S CABLE TELEVISION MONITOR, Nov. 1, 1993, at 3.

21. *Municipally Owned Cable Television Systems*, PUBLIC POWER, Jan.-Feb. 1993, at 156.

systems encompass about 108,000 subscribers. Although many are small, a few have more than 10,000 subscribers.[22] According to one report, "Dozens of local regulatory authorities are considering building their own cable systems . . . aided by program access and other provisions of 1992 Cable Act, and pushed by consumers angered by double-digit cable rate increases."[23]

The involvement of electric utilities in cable television stems in part from the attraction of using existing rights of way. But perhaps more important are the possibilities of using their transmission systems for electricity load management. A leading example is the system—called the fully interactive communications and control system (FICCS)—operated by the Glasgow Electric Power Board in Glasgow, Kentucky, in competition with a privately owned cable system.[24]

The initial intent of the Glasgow system . . . was simply to find new and better ways to manage its distribution network and monitor consumption to reduce energy costs to consumers. The primary application of the network was, and still is, for load management and communication for the utility's supervisory control and data acquisition system.[25]

The Glasgow system "will allow continuous information to flow to the consumers explaining how the program can help them lower their energy bills."[26]

Cable ownership by municipalities and municipally owned electric utilities raises two troublesome issues. First, if a market exists for power load management through use of broadband cable transmission,

22. For example, Conway, Arkansas; San Bruno, California; and Frankfort, Kentucky, counted respectively 10,832; 11,450; and 15,853 subscribers. *Id.*

23. WARREN'S CABLE REGULATION MONITOR, Feb. 1, 1993, at 1.

24. GLASGOW ELECTRIC PLANT BOARD, GLASGOW'S FULLY INTERACTIVE COMMUNICATIONS & CONTROL SYSTEM (1993) [hereinafter GLASGOW REPORT]. As of June 30, 1993, after four years of operation, the system had 1,745 subscribers out of about 6,000 households. *Id.,* pt. 2, question 13.

25. Bob Bruce, *The Lure of Fiber Optics*, PUBLIC POWER, Sept.-Oct. 1993, at 16, 18.

26. GLASGOW REPORT, *supra* note 24, at pt. 2, question 3.

why don't today's privately owned cable systems offer this service? With the pressures faced by cable operators to make best use of their channel capacity, surely they would be anxious to tap this new revenue source. Unfortunately, the use of cable systems for energy load management is handicapped by the lack of a low-cost interface between the customer's electric meter and the TV set-top converter. As noted in Glasgow,

> There is a need for a more cost effective solution to allow an electric meter to report its readings back via the broadband interface . . . . The City of Glasgow, on its own, does not have the resources to pay for such an interface to be custom built for FICCS.[27]

Perhaps the greatest contribution of electric utility involvement in cable is its demonstration of the market potential for suitable interfaces. When, and if, such equipment is developed, we can reasonably expect private owned cable systems to respond to the new opportunities, with electric utilities, as well as residential subscribers, counted among the customers. The use of cable for energy load management will provide no strong rationale for electric utility *ownership* of cable systems.

Moreover, publicly owned entities have certain advantages that do not reflect any inherent economic efficiency but are precisely of the sort that should be avoided in the design of ground rules for future competition.

- Publicly owned entities are accorded tax advantages not available to private firms. Although some pay "in-lieu-of" taxes as a substitute for property taxes,[28] as nonprofit entities they do not pay income taxes.

- They have undue access to lower costs of capital. Because the

---

27. *Id.*, at pt. 2, question 15.

28. Telephone Interview with William J. Ray, Superintendent, Glasgow Electric Plant Board (Oct. 7, 1993).

incremental cost of capital for cable ventures is greater than that for much less risky electric utility activities, for example, diversification of the utility into cable television tends to raise the cost of capital. Unless cable revenues are sufficient to cover this higher incremental cost, monopoly ratepayers are forced to subsidize the utility's cable ventures through higher rates.[29]

- Public entities may subsidize construction and operation with tax dollars. As one example, the municipally owned Paragould, Arkansas, system is reported to be subsidized by $23 of property taxes per household annually.[30]

- Public entities may not have the same franchise obligations as those imposed on privately owned incumbents. Especially, exemptions may be granted from payment of franchise fees, which can amount to as much as 5 percent of gross cable revenues.

- Public entities may unfairly exercise government powers, including zoning and permits, not afforded to private competitors.

These factors imply that the true resource costs to society of entry into cable television through overbuilding by publicly owned entities may be higher than initially appears.

Conclusions

All in all, the prospects for widespread cable overbuilding are not bright. The economics are questionable, given the high investment requirements and possibilities of strategic behavior by the incumbent.

---

29. Of course, concern about cross-subsidization through the capital market is not limited to publicly owned enterprises. The same problem arises with respect to privately owned electric utilities diversifying into risky ventures, as well as the LECs' entry into video.

30. WARREN'S CABLE TELEVISION MONITOR, Nov. 1, 1993, at 3.

The 1992 Cable Act will probably help only marginally in reducing the difficulties confronted by newcomers in gaining franchise approval. Moreover, widespread entry by municipalities would be met with complaints by the investor-owned cable industry of unfair competition, which might trigger remedial legislative action.

A key difficulty for overbuilders is that their technologies (coaxial cable and fiber) and their service offerings are essentially the same as those available to the incumbent. The prospects for successful entry would be improved if the newcomer could exploit economies of scope in offering multiple services not now available to cable subscribers. For this reason, whatever widespread wireline competition emerges will more likely come from the LECs, seeking to offer telephone and video services together, than from electric utilities and other entities treated here.

A remaining concern is the provision in the 1992 Cable Act that mandates uniform pricing by the cable operator in the franchise area. As long emphasized in the telecommunications pricing literature, the firm must have the freedom to cut prices in response to competition, subject to the constraint that price for the service be sufficiently high to generate enough revenue to cover at least its incremental cost.[31] In contrast, a uniform price rule encourages uneconomic entry. The newcomer may thrive not because its costs for a given output are lower than those of the incumbent but only because its costs are lower than the incumbent's minimum uniform (or franchise-wide) price. Uniform price requirements will contribute to economic inefficiencies by handicapping incumbent cable operators from meeting competition not only from overbuilders of concern here, but also from the LECs, wireless cable, and other sources discussed later.

---

31. For a detailed discussion, see WILLIAM J. BAUMOL & J. GREGORY SIDAK, TOWARD COMPETITION IN LOCAL TELEPHONY 49-60 (MIT Press/AEI Press 1994).

3

The Technology and Economics of
Entry by Local Telephone Companies

THE HIGHLY SUCCESSFUL development and commercialization of fiber-optic transmission technology have encouraged widespread optimism that the LECs will emerge as powerful competitors to cable companies. According to this view, construction of fiber-based integrated broadband networks will enable the LECs to combine telephone and video services as a lower-cost substitute for existing copper telephone lines and coaxial television cables. Moreover, as many argue, the vast capacity afforded by fiber will open the way to a host of new two-way interactive services.

Indeed, the interest expressed in expanding the use of fiber to strengthen the nation's communications infrastructure is nothing short of astounding. George Keyworth, former White House science adviser, concludes that "the single most important thing that the U.S. could do now to promote U.S. industrial interests is to speed the wiring up of this country with a fiber optic communications network."[1] Alfred Sikes, former FCC chairman, has stated, "I believe our tax laws should be carefully examined to make sure that we are, at the very least, providing a favorable tax environment for building fiber-based networks to every home and business in this nation."[2] According to

1. GEORGE A. KEYWORTH II & BRUCE ABELL, COMPETITIVENESS & TELECOMMUNICATIONS 21 (Hudson Inst. 1990).
2. Alfred C. Sikes, The Future of Interactive Communications, Address Before the Annual Business Week Symposium on Information Highways (Sept. 11, 1991).

George Gilder, "Fiber optics is a technology of such stunning potential that it will soon overthrow the previous relationship between fast computers and slow wires."[3] He further observes that "this new world of computer communications will break down into two domains—the fibersphere and the atmosphere."[4]

Sharing this optimism, U S West has announced its intention to construct fiber networks across its entire fourteen-state service area.[5] Pacific Bell has announced a plan for investing $16 billion in California "to upgrade its core network infrastructure over the next seven years and to begin building an integrated telecommunications information and entertainment network providing advanced voice, data and video services."[6] Bell Atlantic plans an "enhanced" network that will pass 8.75 million homes in its territory by the end of the year 2000.[7]

Contrary to widely voiced expectations, however, the LECs will face great difficulty in competing with incumbent cable operators—at least during the remainder of this decade. The primary reasons are that (1) cable operators already pass more than 95 percent of the nation's homes with broadband coaxial cable,[8] (2) they can more easily upgrade their networks with fiber than the LECs can for expanded broadband services, and (3) cable operators can more readily exploit the economies of scope in combining video and telephone services on the same network. Whatever near-term competition emerges between the LECs and incumbent cable operators is at least as likely to involve telephony as video services.

Conceivably, continuing technological progress will drive down

3. George Gilder, *Into the Fibersphere*, FORBES ASAP, Dec. 7, 1992, at 111, 111.

4. George Gilder, *Telecosm, The New Rule of Wireless*, FORBES ASAP, Mar. 29, 1993, at 96, 96.

5. U S West, *U S West Communications to Build Mass-Market Video Network*, Press Release, Feb. 4, 1993.

6. Pacific Bell, *Pacific Bell Invests in California's Communications Superhighway*, Press Release, Nov. 11, 1993, at 1.

7. Bell Atlantic, *Bell Atlantic Accelerates Network Deployment*, Press Release, Dec. 1, 1993, at 1.

8. Of the 93 million television households reported at the end of 1992, cable networks passed 89.4 million, or about 96 percent. NATIONAL CABLE TELEVISION ASS'N, CABLE TELEVISION DEVELOPMENTS 1-A (Mar. 1993).

network investment cost to such a small part of the total cost for video services (which also includes operations and maintenance, administration, programming, and marketing) that LECs could compete successfully even if forced to duplicate transmission facilities. But such advances cannot reasonably be expected, if they occur at all, before the next century. The near-term prospects for the LECs would be markedly improved if they find a way to use their existing copper facilities for satisfactory delivery of video.

Despite the first-mover advantages of cable operators, the LECs have good reason to probe the potential offered by video as part of their diversified portfolios of new business activities. Strategic alliances between the LECs (through their parent telephone companies), cable MSOs, and others will be important—perhaps critical—in pursuing whatever opportunities do emerge in the video market.

Exploration of the LECs' potential role in video markets, from which these and other conclusions are drawn, is the task of this chapter and the following two. In this chapter, we assume that the LECs have the same freedom to participate in the video market as do today's cable operators. That is, they may carry their own video programming and control the content of information carried over their channels. With this assumption, we focus on likely outcomes as affected by available technologies, expected costs, and prospective markets for existing and new services. Accordingly, this chapter is divided into six topics: (1) the role of fiber optics, (2) cable entry into telephony, (3) use of digital video compression, (4) use of existing copper networks, (5) effects of longer-term technological advances, (6) prospects for new services, and (7) the LECs' motivations for video entry in light of the preceding discussion.

The Role of Fiber Optics

Both cable operators and LECs are using fiber to upgrade their networks. For telephone service alone, some LECs are installing fiber from the central offices to remote distribution units and from there are using conventional copper local loops to connect subscriber premises. This application, called the digital loop carrier, is a straightforward way to reduce costs by aggregating telephone traffic between numerous subscribers and the central office.

Similarly, many cable operators are substituting fiber for coaxial cable in their trunk lines. In tree-and-branch fashion, trunk lines carry signals to coaxial distribution lines that, in turn, link into the drop cables connected to individual subscribers. Substituted for coaxial cable, fiber improves reception quality, reduces maintenance costs, improves reliability, and expands channel capacity. Fiber installations in cable systems grew from near zero in 1988 to more than 24,000 route miles by the end of 1992.[9]

Thus, for both the LECs and cable operators, the issue is not whether to introduce fiber into the local network for broadband service but rather *how far* to extend it. Beyond fiber in their trunks, cable operators generally favor extension of fiber into the distribution network, called fiber to the neighborhood or fiber to the node. At the node (perhaps an underground vault) the transmission is converted from light to electrical signals. From each node, conventional coaxial feeders and drop lines serve some hundreds of subscribers. As an example, in 1992, Time Warner put into experimental operation in Queens, New York, a 150-channel system—twice the capacity of its network before the fiber upgrade.[10] Some LECs as well have proposed this architecture in section 214 applications filed with the Commission.[11]

Interest has also been widely expressed in extending fiber closer to the home. A leading candidate is fiber to the curb, whereby fiber is brought to a curbside vault, from which a dozen or so homes could be served with conventional coaxial lines. The first full-scale commercial applications of fiber for integrated video and telephone (both involving

---

9. PAUL KAGAN ASSOCIATES, CABLE TV TECHNOLOGY, Mar. 19, 1993, at 1. A useful tutorial on cable technology and network design is contained in RICHARD BILOTTI, JR., DREW HANSON & RICHARD J. MACDONALD, THE CABLE TELEVISION INDUSTRY: NEW TECHNOLOGIES, NEW OPPORTUNITIES AND NEW COMPETITION (Grantchester Sec. & Wasserstein Perella Sec., Mar. 8, 1993).

10. Sharon D. Moshavi, *Time Warner Unveils 150 Channels*, BROADCASTING, Dec. 23, 1991, at 18.

11. See generally the section 214 applications of Ameritech, Pacific Bell, and U S West for commercial video dialtone service, on file with the Commission as of February 1994.

fiber to the curb) were proposed in late 1992 by Bell Atlantic for two areas in New Jersey.[12]

In earlier years, there was much talk among LECs about extending fiber all the way to the home. For the near term, however, this approach is generally regarded as too expensive.[13] The advantage of fiber only to the curb lies in the sharing of costly electronic equipment among a number of households. Electronics sharing is practical to an even greater degree with fiber to the neighborhood.

If LECs installed fiber only to the neighborhood, they would still face the task of getting video to the home, because their existing copper networks cannot carry broadband signals. By running fiber all the way to the curb, they would need to install only relatively short coaxial drop lines to reach individual homes—but still at the expense of replacing their narrowband networks. In contrast, cable operators can use their existing coaxial cable networks to reach the home from more-distant neighborhood nodes. This circumstance gives them an advantage over the LECs. At moderate cost, they can extend fiber into the neighborhood and still use much of their existing local distribution networks, while the LECs must replace virtually their entire local copper plant to install fiber either to the neighborhood or to the curb.

To estimate the costs of these alternative approaches is difficult because of uncertainty in the face of rapid technological progress. A bewildering array of cost estimates has been advanced by LECs, manufacturers, and others—but generally without explanation of underlying assumptions or sufficient detail to enable independent assessment of reliability. In response, we draw heavily from the analysis of David Reed, who has provided the most carefully documented estimates available for network costs in the mid- to late

12. New Jersey Bell, FCC Section 214 Applications for Dover Township, W-P-C 6840 (Dec. 15, 1992) [hereinafter Dover Section 214 Application]; New Jersey Bell, FCC Section 214 Applications for Florham Park Borough, Madison Borough, and Chatham Borough, W-P-C 6838 (Nov. 16, 1992) [hereinafter Florham Park Section 214 Application].

13. Carol Wilson, *Bellcore Revisits the Residential Broadband Cost Question*, TELEPHONY, July 26, 1993, at 9-16.

1990s,[14] supplemented by other sources.

We start by noting that the cost of rebuilding an existing cable system with fiber to the neighborhood is estimated in one study at about $250 to $300 per subscriber.[15] For new "model" networks, Reed estimates a much higher cost in a fiber-to-the-curb system that combines telephone and video service. The two network architectures he describes have estimated investment costs of $1,242 and $1,222 per home passed. With an assumed sign-up rate of 60 percent for video subscribers, the per subscriber cost would amount to about $2,000.[16] In contrast, another source estimates an outlay of only $1,150 per subscriber for a LEC-provided integrated network. The assumptions underlying this estimate, however, are unclear.[17]

To be sure, with more fiber in the network, a fiber-to-the-curb system may have greater potential capacity than a cable upgrade to the neighborhood. The key question is, What do subscribers want and are willing to pay for? Fiber to the neighborhood can supply 150 channels (illustrated by the Time Warner system in Queens noted earlier), and a few hundred channels can be added with digital compression, as discussed below. Conceivably, a strong market would exist for even greater capacity, if, for example, multitudes of residential customers in a local geographical area simultaneously wanted immediate access to separate programs stored in a central electronic library. In this case, installation of broadband switching to connect individual subscribers to program sources along with fiber closer to the home—perhaps to the curb—would be economically justified. But, even here, the cable operator would have no *disadvantage* vis-à-vis the LEC. In the extreme case of enormous residential demands for capacity, both would be obliged to replace most or all of their existing networks, along with needing access to broadband switching.

Yet, the LEC is commonly regarded as having an advantage by virtue of its ability to enjoy the economies of scope in combining video

14. DAVID P. REED, RESIDENTIAL FIBER OPTIC NETWORKS, AN ENGINEERING AND ECONOMIC ANALYSIS (Artech House 1992).

15. *See* BILOTTI, HANSON & MACDONALD, *supra* note 9, at 36.

16. REED, *supra* note 14, at 298-301.

17. PAUL KAGAN ASSOCIATES, *supra* note 9, at 1.

and telephone services. The extent of these economies, however, depends on particular network architectures. Moreover, whatever scope economies arise are likely to be as easily exploited by cable operators as by LECs.

To illustrate, recall the per-subscriber investment of $2,000 noted above for a fiber-to-the-curb system for telephony and video. Scope economies would be indicated only if the sum of the costs of providing telephony and video separately exceeds this figure. A free-standing telephone digital loop carrier network is estimated at about $690 per subscriber,[18] while a conventional cable system runs to about $700 per subscriber.[19] The figure of $700 rises to $1,000 if the $300 estimated earlier is added to upgrade the system with fiber to the neighborhood. The sum of the two stand-alone costs—$690 and $1,000—is *less* than, not greater than, the $2,000 estimated for the integrated system.

This result is counterinteractive. Why should it cost more to add either telephony or video to an integrated system than to build a separate network? Surely opportunities exist for cost savings in combining services on common facilities, such as on fiber cables themselves. The explanation lies in the apparent fact that fiber to the curb is not the optimal configuration for providing telephone service alone, and, as emphasized above, it would be the optimal configuration for video service only if subscriber demand for channel capacity were very high.

To elaborate, the cost of fiber-to-the-curb architecture is driven by the high cost of decentralized electronics in the curbside vaults.[20] Among the elements contributing to the high cost, the need to maintain universally available and dependable telephone service handicaps the integration of services on fiber to the curb. Most notably, the need to provide emergency power, although at first blush seeming like a trivial

---

18. REED, *supra* note 14, at 288-89.

19. Competition, Rate Deregulation, and the Commission's Policies Relating to the Provision of Cable Television Service, Report, MM Dkt. No. 89-600, 5 F.C.C. Rcd. 4962, 5076 n.11 (1990).

20. In the cases Reed describes, electronics are responsible for more than 50 percent of total system cost. *See* REED, *supra* note 16.

task, presents serious difficulties. Today, telephone copper lines themselves are used to conduct electricity for normal and emergency power from the central office to the subscriber's telephone. Since fiber does not conduct electricity, however, a new source of emergency power is needed. One obvious possibility, the use of rechargeable batteries, is expensive and technically troublesome. A leading alternative is the continued use of copper lines from the central office to provide power. But if copper is used to conduct electricity, why not use the same lines to provide telephone service as well? In contrast, emergency power is more easily provided at the more centralized neighborhood node, from which the power can be distributed to some hundreds of homes by existing copper line.[21]

Quite possibly, some subscribers would choose to forgo access to emergency power if doing so would permit service at lower rates. If emergency power is to be brought to the neighborhood node for those who opt for it, however, the additional cost to the LEC of supplying power to the rest would be small. Only if all households sharing the node agree to forgo emergency power would substantial cost savings accrue.

The prospects for the LECs would be brighter if fiber to the curb improved the quality of basic telephone service. Except for a possible reduction in operating and maintenance expenses,[22] however, the extension of fiber to the curb would not notably benefit subscribers who continue to want only basic service.

The lack of benefits to telephone users lies at the heart of concerns about cross-subsidization posed by LEC entry into video. As discussed in Chapter 4, basic telephone ratepayers stand to lose, it is widely argued, because the LECs may shift some costs of video service to telephone users, resulting in higher telephone rates. Concerns about cross-subsidization would be less pressing if telephone users could be shown to benefit from replacement of the existing network with integrated broadband facilities.

---

21. For a discussion of powering, with many cites to the technical literature, see *id.* at 96-102.

22. *Id.* at 133-35.

In contrast to the above results, marked economies of scope may well exist for fiber-to-the-neighborhood architectures, where the high cost of electronic equipment can be shared among larger numbers of subscribers. Reed estimates that total investment cost for such a network may run to about $1,130 per subscriber for video service alone.[23] Adding telephone service may involve an additional $280—far below the stand-alone estimate of a digital carrier system of $690 noted earlier.[24] Expressed differently, the estimate of $1,410 ($1,130 + $280) for the integrated network is smaller than the sum of estimated stand-alone costs of $690 and $1,000 noted earlier.

Cable Entry into Telephony

These numbers suggest that cable operators may more easily compete with the LECs in telephony than the LECs can in video. Unless the demand for video channel capacity is large, as previously noted, the installation of fiber to the neighborhood is a better choice than the extension of fiber to the curb. For video service, cable operators have a comparative advantage over the LECs in installing fiber to the neighborhood because they can continue to use a larger portion of their existing networks. Moreover, with this architecture, cable operators may be able to supply telephone service, at least in limited volumes, at low cost.

The fundamental factor driving these relationships is the ability of copper coaxial cable to carry both broadband and narrowband signals, while LEC local copper lines are limited to narrowband transmission. If the integrated broadband network to the home does emerge, it may trace its beginnings to the cable industry rather than to the telephone industry.[25]

23. David P. Reed, *The Prospects for Competition in the Subscriber Loop: The Fiber to the Neighborhood Approach*, Presented at the Twenty-First Annual Telecommunications Policy Research Policy Conference 19 (Sept. 1993).

24. *Id.*

25. For additional support of this possible outcome, see Paul Baran, The Universal Communications System of the Future: Telephone or TV Cable?, Address Before the NCTA Cable Convention (June 8, 1993).

Several telephone markets hold promise for cable operators. The emerging market for personal communications services (PCS) has attracted special interest.[26] These services will provide wireless links to individuals equipped with vest-pocket portable telephones. The primary advantage over today's cellular telephony is lower subscriber cost. With the addition of switches, cable networks may be upgradable for switched telephone traffic more generally. The provision of switched narrowband services by cable operators would be facilitated by switching services purchased from the LECs. Cable operators, as well as other LEC competitors, stand to benefit from the FCC's rules for expanded interconnection of competing carriers for interstate services and from moves of some states to facilitate interconnection for intrastate services.[27]

In addition to the alliances noted in Chapter 1, numerous cable operators are entering into ventures to facilitate entry into telephone markets. Comcast has acquired Metromedia's cellular telephone interests, placing Comcast "among the nation's top five non-wireline cellular operators."[28] Continental Cablevision of Jacksonville, Florida, and Hyperion Telecommunications have agreed to form a joint venture that will take advantage of Continental's existing fiber-optic lines. The infrastructure will be expanded to deliver "local access telephone voice and data connections between Jacksonville-area commercial customers and interexchange carriers."[29] In late 1993, five of the largest cable MSOs agreed to form a joint venture to offer PCS and other special-

---

26. For a technical and economic analysis of PCS, including the potential role of cable operators and LECs, see DAVID P. REED, PUTTING IT ALL TOGETHER: THE COST STRUCTURE OF PERSONAL COMMUNICATIONS SERVICES (FCC Office of Plans & Policy Working Paper No. 28, 1992).

27. *See* Expanded Interconnection with Local Telephone Company Facilities, Report and Order, and Notice of Proposed Rulemaking, CC Dkt. Nos. 91-141, 92-222, 7 F.C.C. Rcd. 7369 (1992) (adopting rules for expanded interconnection for special access services); Expanded Interconnection with Local Telephone Company Facilities, Second Report and Order, and Third Notice of Proposed Rulemaking, CC Dkt. Nos. 91-141, 80-286, 8 F.C.C. Rcd. 7374 (1993) (adopting rules of expanded interconnection for switched access); NATIONAL ASS'N OF REGULATORY UTILITY COMMISSIONERS, THE STATUS OF COMPETITION IN INTRASTATE TELECOMMUNICATIONS 174 (1993).

28. TELECOMMUNICATIONS REP., Mar. 9, 1992, at 21.

29. TELECOMMUNICATIONS REP., May 18, 1992, at 37.

ized telecommunications services in metropolitan areas.[30] According to early plans, the "national venture will serve as an umbrella organization providing marketing, operational, and support services to separately incorporated local joint ventures."[31] Local services will be provided through Teleport Communications Group—a provider of business telecommunications services in competition with LECs in major U.S. cities. Teleport is to be wholly owned by the five MSOs, with TCI and Cox collectively holding a 50 percent share.[32]

All this is not to imply that cable entry into telephony will be easy. In addition to government regulatory hurdles, cable operators face potential technical difficulties in providing narrowband services. The tree-and-branch cable topology may be susceptible to signal interference that, without costly upgrading, could reduce the quality of telephone service to unacceptable levels. Further, the ability of cable networks to supply telephone service at today's high levels of reliability remains to be assessed. Finally, difficulties may emerge in provision of custom calling features on tree-and-branch networks.[33]

Digital Video Compression

This new technology, which has generated widespread interest by both cable operators and LECs, would further expand capacity in conjunction with fiber and coaxial cable. Signal compression takes advantage of the fact that only portions of a television picture change from frame to frame. By transmitting only the information (measured in bits per second) needed for frame-to-frame changes, compression permits several channels to be derived from the bandwidth of a single conventional channel, depending on the nature of the programming. A fast-

---

30. These include Comcast Corp., Continental Cablevision, Inc., Cox Cable Communications, and Time Warner Entertainment Co. L.P. *See* TELECOMMUNICATIONS REP., Dec. 6, 1993, at 3-4.

31. *Id.* at 3.

32. *Id.*

33. Reed, *supra* note 23, at 13-14. For a description of an integrated telephony/video system now being offered for commercial use, see Scientific Atlanta, CoAccess, CATV Telephone System (Nov. 1993).

moving sports event is more demanding of bandwidth than a head-and-shoulders interview. A live-action scene, covered at thirty frames per second by a video camera, requires a greater information transmission flow (hence bandwidth) than the same scene stored on film and shown at twenty-four frames per second.[34] In all cases, equipment is required to compress individual signals, and decoders are needed for each television set to decompress the signals and to convert them from digital to analog for viewer presentation.

Cable operators generally favor a hybrid approach under which digital transmission and compression are added to existing analog channels on the same network. TCI's plans for upgraded service, reported in early 1993, call for 550 MHz of bandwidth devoted to current analog service and 200 MHz to digitally compressed channels, with later upgrades extending to 1 GHz.[35] Thus, a cable system with an original capacity of, say, sixty analog channels might be upgraded to 500 channels, with the additional channels delivered by digital transmission and signal compression.[36] Presumably, subscribers would pay about as much as they do today for analog service, while digitally compressed offerings would be offered at an additional charge. The success of digital transmission and video compression will critically depend not only on subscriber demand, but also on the cost of the decoders—all the more so since a decoder is needed for each television set that receives digital service.

Use of Existing Copper Networks

The prospects for widespread LEC entry into the video market would be brighter if LECs could find a way to use their existing copper

34. Earl E. Manchester, *New Uses for Residential Copper*, TELEPHONY, June 10, 1991, at 34.

35. WARREN'S CABLE REGULATION MONITOR, Apr. 19, 1993, at 4.

36. BILOTTI, HANSON & MACDONALD, *supra* note 9, at 47. In their analysis, Bilotti, Hanson, and MacDonald assume a channel multiplication ratio of five-to-one for compressed signals, which yields 450 digitally compressed channels along with 60 analog signals. *See also* CRAIG K. TANNER, DIGITAL COMPRESSION AND TRANSMISSION (Cable Television Lab., Nov. 1992); STEPHEN D. DUKES, NEXT GENERATION CABLE NETWORK ARCHITECTURE (Cable Television Lab., Apr. 1992).

networks to carry broadband signals. An approach now under field test involves asynchronous digital subscriber line (ADSL) technology, which uses a advanced form of signal compression to enable the existing copper drop line to carry one or more television signals, along with telephone service, to the subscriber.[37] Each television set connected to ADSL service would have a decoder that decompresses the digital signal and converts it to analog. The single video channel to which the television set has access would be switched at the central office, or at another central point, for subscriber access to all program sources. Thus, the subscriber would receive pay per view, pay per channel, and other offerings through a central switch connected to a digital file server. The capacity of the single switched channel would be limited only by the number of program choices available at the server.

This application of switched video contrasts with today's distributed video cable service, where all the programs carried on the cable system pass the household, with the subscriber using a set-top converter to choose the particular channel to be viewed. Potentially, the single-channel switched system has many times the capacity of even the most advanced distributive system (for example, 500 channels) now on the drawing boards.

Extreme differences of opinion exist about the technical feasibility and economics of ADSL technology for widespread use, with some LECs proceeding with plans for field testing, and others dismissing this approach. Bell Atlantic is testing an ADSL system, initially involving several hundred of its employees, in northern Virginia.[38] It is also proposing a full-scale ADSL system to pass 300,000 homes in the Maryland and Virginia suburbs of Washington, D.C.[39] In contrast, in its plans for entering the video arena, Pacific Bell is reported to regard

37. E. Stephen Fleming & Michael B. McLaughlin, *ADSL: The On-Ramp to the Information Highway*, TELEPHONY, July 12, 1993, at 20-26.

38. Chesapeake & Potomac Tel. Co. of Va., FCC Section 214 Application, W-P-C-6834 (Oct. 21, 1992) [hereinafter *C&P Telephone Section 214 Application*].

39. C&P Telephone Companies of Virginia and Maryland, FCC Section 214 Application, W-P-C-6912 (Dec. 16, 1993).

ADSL as "a high-cost, niche technology."[40] Numerous factors account for wide differences of opinion about the potential of ADSL. The following are among the most important.

Reception Quality. Current ADSL experiments involve a bit stream of 1.5 Mbps per video channel. This speed is sufficient only for videocassette recorder (VCR)–like reception with programming shot on film at twenty-four frames per second. A higher bit stream of 3 Mbps would be required for typical live presentations shot at thirty frames per second, and 6 Mbps would be required for presentation of fast-action scenes, including live sporting events.[41] Technical problems are exacerbated by the requirement that the copper line carry more than one video channel, if multiple television receivers in the household are to be served at the same time (with different signals). The bit stream capacity of the copper line varies inversely with distance. A high bit stream—higher than 6 Mbps—can be carried over short distances, based on current and near-term technological developments. But capacity is much more constrained at the distances of two to three miles characteristic of the lengths of residential local loops from the LEC central office.[42] The condition of individual local loops also affects performance. Although old copper could be replaced with new, doing so would undercut the attraction that ADSL holds for using existing networks. Unless ADSL can be perfected to carry the full range of television programming including live sports, LECs using this approach would be handicapped in competing with cable service.

Cost. The cost of subscriber equipment to decompress signals and to perform ancillary tasks is uncertain. To be competitive with cable, the cost of ADSL equipment would have to fall well below the $600 to $700 typically quoted for investment per cable subscriber. Moreover, ADSL systems would have to offer many hundreds of program choices. The cost of video servers with such capacities is also uncertain. The server proposed by Bell Atlantic for its field testing will

40. WARREN'S CABLE TELEVISION MONITOR, Apr. 12, 1993, at 5.

41. Fred Dawson, *Telco Video*, CABLEVISION, Sept. 9, 1991, at 32-33.

42. Carol Wilson & Richard Karpinski, *Telcos Press Vendors for Video Solutions—Now*, TELEPHONY, Apr. 26, 1993, at 8.

store about 400 full-length movies at a cost of $12 million.[43] How costs will scale with capacity, how many subscribers will be accessed from a single server, and how continuing technological advances and volume production will affect costs are yet to be determined.

Signal Interference. Similar to potential problems of offering telephone service on cable systems, interference may pose a problem in use of ordinary telephone copper line for broadband service. The varying gauges of wire used in telephone distribution plant, imperfections in splicing, and installation anomalies (which cause no problem in ordinary telephone use) could prove troublesome in a new transmission environment. Especially, whether the wiring inside the home will be susceptible to interference from household electrical appliances and other sources is unclear. The need for costly cable retrofitting and other remedial measures would undercut the appeal of ADSL, whose favorable economics depend on using existing plant essentially as is.

The Electronic Video Store? Suppose that (1) the preceding problems are shown to be tractable, (2) the investment cost for ADSL is low (say, no more than $300), and (3) reception remains at only VCR quality suitable for stored programming. In this case, the greatest potential for ADSL might be in competing with videocassette stores rather than directly with cable. Thus, for the same reasons that many cable subscribers also rent or purchase videocassettes, they would, as a substitute, be attracted to ADSL service. In this case, although not directly competitive with cable, ADSL applications would tap a rich market. Rentals and sales of videocassettes have skyrocketed, from $5 billion in 1986 to $12 billion in 1992.[44] This latest figure is nearly one-half of total cable industry revenues, which ran to $25 billion in 1992.[45] The possibility of siphoning off video store revenues, by itself, provides an incentive for the LECs, through field trials and other means, to explore the potential of ADSL.

---

43. *C&P Telephone Section 214 Application, supra* note 38.

44. BILOTTI, HANSON & MACDONALD, *supra* note 9, at 21.

45. NATIONAL CABLE TELEVISION ASS'N, *supra* note 8, at 8-A, 8-B. This figure includes cable advertising revenues.

Longer-Term Technological Advances

The preceding assessment has concentrated primarily on likely outcomes during the remainder of this century. In the longer term, technological advances could alter the above relationships to render more economically feasible competition by the LECs with cable operators. With sufficient decline in fiber network costs, the prospects for successful competitive entry into video would be driven not by network costs but by its ability to contain marketing, administrative, and other expenses, while adding new or improved services. In other words, with cost relationships altered as a consequence of technological advance, the first-mover advantage held by cable operators during the 1990s would disappear. With wireline networks becoming so inexpensive, the LECs, and possibly other entities, could successfully compete in the wireline video market.

It is impossible to predict when, or whether, this outcome will emerge. The best that can be said is that during this decade, at least, network investment costs will continue to loom as a substantial fraction of total costs for wireline video delivery. As evidence, the experience of cable operators is relevant. Table 3–1 displays a sample of cable operating expenses. To obtain an estimate of total cost, we must include network investment. The $700 per subscriber investment for a conventional cable system, noted earlier, involves an annualized cost of about $112, given an assumed pre-tax rate of return of 15 percent and a twenty-year useful life.

This figure is 35 percent of total cost, consisting of $204 in operating costs plus $112 in the annualized cost of network investment.[46] As networks are upgraded with fiber and video compression, this investment cost will rise, as discussed earlier. At the same time, programming and marketing costs will also probably rise (reflecting the use of more channels). With the network architectures and technologies now being incorporated in LEC—and cable operator—investment plans, network investment costs will remain a substantial portion of total costs

---

46. Another cost study estimates that annual operating expenses for a "typical" urban cable system run to about $188, slightly lower than for the sample in Table 3-1. *See* T. BALDWIN & D. McVOY, CABLE COMMUNICATION 417 (Prentice-Hall 1988).

TABLE 3-1
CABLE OPERATING EXPENSES PER SUBSCRIBER,
SAMPLE OF CABLE SYSTEMS, 1990

Category	*Amount ($)*	*Percent*
General and administrative	59	29
Marketing	26	13
Technical[a]	46	23
Programming	73	36
Total	204	100

a. Includes network operations and maintenance.
SOURCE: CONTINENTAL CABLEVISION, INC., CABLE TELEVISION OPERATIONS AND
FINANCE (seminar for FCC staff, Mar. 26, 1990).

during this decade. Even if technological advances dramatically reduced network costs later in this decade, the time required to bring these advances from the laboratory to the manufacturing plant would push widespread commercialization into the next century.

Moreover, technological advances that reduce network costs (such as improved video compression techniques) will benefit other transmission modes as well—direct broadcast satellites and terrestrial wireless systems. We cannot predict how competitive relationships between LECs and other video providers would evolve in such a future of crosscurrents, other than to say that, surely, the American public would have access to dramatically larger volumes of information than it does now.

New Services

The LECs emphasize that fiber-based integrated networks will enable them to provide a host of new services. As one example, in its

TABLE 3-2
PROPOSED NEW SERVICES OF NEW JERSEY BELL, 1992

Single channel video	Formal education
Video gaming	Travel services
Interactive data base	Other concierge
Telecommuting	Medical
Catalog shopping	Financial services
Grocery shopping	Neighborhood net
Multimedia library	Music video
"How to" instructional	

SOURCE: *Dover Section 214 Application, supra* note 12, at attach. B. The application contains no description of these projected services. For a discussion, see Leland L. Johnson, New Jersey Cable Television Association, Reply to Opposition to Petition of the New Jersey Cable Television Association to Deny, W-P-C 6840 (Feb. 17, 1993), at ex. E.

section 214 application for video dialtone service to Dover, New Jersey, New Jersey Bell has estimated that 59 percent of its broadband revenues in the year 2002 will come from services of the sort not now provided by cable operators, as shown in Table 3-2.[47]

On-Demand Switched Video. A widely referenced potential service is on-demand video, whereby a subscriber would have access to movies and other materials in an electronic version of today's video rental store. As afforded also by ADSL applications already discussed, choices would be available from the hundreds or thousands of programs stored in a video server at a central location. With a channel dedicated to the use of a single subscriber, enabled by the high-capacity fiber link combined with signal compression to the video server, the subscriber could exercise the same control (exact time of showing, pause, fast forward) as with a VCR.

47. *Dover Section 214 Application, supra* note 12, at ex. 4, attach. B.

The prospects of the LECs greatly depend on what cable operators are doing in the meantime. With more limited use of fiber (to the neighborhood) and with signal compression, cable operators could offer staggered or near on-demand video as a close substitute for the LEC's fully switched service. Within the capacity of a hundred (or a few hundred) channels, enough programs could be shown simultaneously to permit viewers a wide range of choices and starting times (but without full VCR–like control).

The key question is whether switched service would attract enough subscriber demand, over and above that for near on-demand video, to cover the additional costs for the required greater transmission capacity, broadband switching, and program storage. If the market for on-demand video is indeed strong, there is no reason to believe that cable operators would be any slower than the LECs to upgrade their networks to provide it. On the contrary, cable operators would continue to have an advantage through their basic broadband network already in place.[48]

All this is not to say that cable operators will have an assured market for their upgraded networks with many dozens or hundreds of channels. They, too, may have a hard time covering the cost of extensive fiber retrofits and the addition of digital compression. But if the market for the cable operators' near on-demand offerings is weak, it is likely to be weak also for the LECs' full on-demand offerings. If cable operators do encounter weak demand, they can postpone or abandon plans for further extensive upgrades and retain their analog service, which is almost universally available and already enjoys a strong market. In contrast, investment cutbacks by the LECs would weaken or eliminate their presence in the video market, since they would not have existing broadband networks to fall back on.

Interactive Services. Much emphasis has been placed by the LECs on a host of interactive services, commonly involving multimedia offerings that mix voice, text, data, and video. High-speed data transfer between home and workplace, enhanced distance learning, tele-

---

48. For additional discussion of the economics of on-demand video, see LELAND L. JOHNSON & DAVID P. REED, RESIDENTIAL BROADBAND SERVICES BY TELEPHONE COMPANIES? 23-28 (RAND 1990).

medicine, teleshopping, and interactive multimedia services are a few examples.

For three reasons, the promise of such services delivered by LECs on fiber is questionable. First, many of these services can be delivered today over cable networks. As one example, in August 1993, Continental Cablevision, the nation's third largest MSO, announced plans to connect its cable customers to the worldwide Internet data network. In cooperation with Performance Systems International (PSI), the plan calls for several channels of television bandwidth to be dedicated to PSI's Internet customers in several regions served by Continental:

> This service will allow households and businesses with a computer and cable TV connection to access the entire suite of Internet data services. These include access to the Library of Congress, international bulletin boards, and unparalleled access to research quality information and data bases. The Internet, the largest data network in the world, now serves over 15 million people with sophisticated services, and connects over 25 million for electronic messages.[49]

In other cases, a telephone uplink for subscriber query or response could be combined for a cable downlink to provide text, graphics, still-frame video, or other presentations. The key problem lies not in a lack of fiber in the network but rather in the high costs of software development in the face of uncertain consumer demand. A range of multimedia offerings, for example, is in the early marketing stage or under development, while new multimedia ventures are proliferating.[50] Problems posed by the complex design and cost of multimedia programming, not transmission capabilities beyond today's networks, are the most serious.

Second, if promising new services do go beyond today's network capabilities, the LECs will have no clear comparative advantage in seizing the opportunity. Consider again interactive multimedia. Both

---

49. Performance Systems Int'l, Inc., *PSI and Continental Cablevision Announce Plans to Deliver Internet over Cable TV*, Press Release, Aug. 1993, at 1.

50. These are routinely reported in *Video Services News* (weekly), among other industry periodicals.

the LECs and cable operators can use fiber and video compression to transmit a combination of voice, text, video, and graphics. With a large emerging market, cable operators could respond more quickly for the same reasons as noted previously: their broadband networks, already passing more than 95 percent of the nation's homes, can be upgraded with fiber and video compression depending on subscriber demand.

Third, both the LECs and cable operators will face competition from nonwireline providers of interactive services. A leading example is development of a wireless data response system for interactive video and data services (IVDS). Developed in the early 1990s, it permits television viewers with special terminals to respond to questions and options shown on television programs. Polling, order taking, and student responses to instructional programs are among the possible applications. After lengthy regulatory proceedings, the FCC decided in 1992 to allocate radio spectrum in each local service area for two competing entities to supply IVDS. The FCC emphasized that IVDS "potentially can provide a multitude of services" and that its decision to allocate twice as much spectrum as it had originally proposed arose from its concern that the smaller allocation "might inhibit the full development of IVDS technology, slow the introduction of services, and thwart the emergence of competitive providers."[51] It is unclear how far IVDS will penetrate the interactive information market. But its potential adds to the risks faced by the LECs in entering this field.

Another system, one that does not necessarily depend on wireline delivery, involves compact disk read-only memory (CD-ROM) devices, which offer many times the information storage capacity of conventional magnetic disks for personal computers. Current development of interactive, computer-based multimedia applications is based largely on this technology. For the residential user, CD-ROM developments may go in two directions. In one, the user buys or rents disks for home use of a player attached to the television set or personal computer. The user could, for example, tap into a library, explore a museum, or take

---

51. TELECOMMUNICATIONS REP., Feb. 24, 1992, at 32. The record of the FCC's deliberations, along with filings by interested parties, is contained in FCC Dkt. No. 91-2.

lessons in calculus, all with a rich variety of interactive text, voice, still-frame video, and full-motion video stored on CDs.

Beyond this closed-circuit application, we can again imagine the electronic version of the video store. The disks and processing equipment would be housed at a server, perhaps at the LEC's central office. Instructed by signals from the incoming subscriber line, programming would be sent back to the subscriber's television set or computer. This mode would permit cost sharing of disks and associated equipment among many users and enable easy access to a wider range of choices than would be available in the home CD inventory. If this application proved attractive, both cable operators and LECs could provide the needed telecommunication links, but again with the cable operator holding an advantage (at least in the near term) for the reasons noted earlier.

Assessment. We would have more reason to be bullish about new services requiring broadband transmission if we could point to examples of resounding success from the numerous experiments and field trials in recent years. In contrast, new exploratory initiatives are typically announced with much fanfare, but, subsequently, we hear rather little about what was actually learned, and whatever does emerge provides no strong grounds for optimism. An example is the experimental cable project involving new services sponsored by GTE in Cerritos, California. The project was started in 1989 after the FCC granted a waiver to its cross-ownership restrictions. It is to be terminated after an FCC decision in November 1993 to rescind the waiver.[52] The notable point here is not the Commission's decision; rather, after several years of experimentation with interactive and other services, little has been officially released about what has been learned. By far the best description—a newspaper account—suggests that

---

52. General Tel. Co. of Cal., Memorandum Opinion and Order on Remand, FCC 93-488, *petition for review docketed sub nom.* GTE California v. FCC, No. 93-70924 (9th Cir. filed Nov. 19, 1993). *See also* TELECOMMUNICATIONS REP., Nov. 15, 1993, at 38-39; General Tel. Co. of Cal., Memorandum Opinion and Order, 8 F.C.C. Rcd. 8753 (1993) (motion for stay of FCC order).

residents in Cerritos expressed little interest in the offerings.[53]

An additional disquieting factor is the tendency to ignore the fact that many existing and contemplated services are partial substitutes for each other. Thus, if interactive games on LEC or cable networks become popular, they will likely cut into the revenues from movies and other entertainment. Yet, it is a common failing in market analysis to project the revenues of a given service, ignoring what else is being offered, and simply add the totals from the individual projections. Both the LECs and cable operators may end up stunned by their overestimates of *net* revenues, stemming from the interdependence among the services.

These concerns do not necessarily portend a disappointing future. The introduction of digital transmission and less expensive technologies for information storage and retrieval could conceivably make a big difference. Still, we have reason for discomfort in seeing so many participants apparently bemused with the attractions of new technologies, to the neglect of hard analysis of likely consumer demand.

Motivations for Market Entry

In view of the questionable near-term prospects for LECs competing with cable operators, why are they, and their parent telephone companies, pushing so hard to enter the video market? There are two explanations. First, some will simply disagree with the preceding analysis on grounds that it overstates the costs and other difficulties faced by the LECs in building integrated networks. Certainly, the high levels of uncertainty provide wide leeway for honest differences of opinion.

Second, and more important, even if the preceding is accepted as a reasonable assessment in light of the uncertainties, a telephone company would have good reason to explore opportunities in video as one element of a diversified business portfolio. Since the AT&T divestiture, conventional wisdom has held that the core telephone

---

53. John Lippman, *Tuning Out the TV of Tomorrow*, L.A. TIMES, Aug. 31, 1993, at 1. This sobering account is recommended reading for anyone interested in telecommunications technologies and prospects for new services.

business would be marked by slow growth because of market maturity and competitive intrusions into traditional monopoly strongholds. It follows that business diversification is critically important to long-term financial health.

The RBOCs have been quick to respond both by line of business (financial services, real estate, software) and by geography (Mexico, Europe, Asia), with mixed success.[54] In their quest for yet other opportunities, the video market offers obvious attractions. Cable industry revenues grew by 14 percent compounded annually during the five-year period from 1987 to 1992, rising to $25 billion—about 30 percent of total local telephone company revenues.[55] Videocassette rentals and sales enjoyed similar rapid growth, as noted. Even if the prospects for near-term competition with incumbent cable operators are problematic, a long-term presence by the LECs in video would neces-sitate actions to achieve a *near*-term presence—evidenced, for example, by ambitious plans for network upgrades, field tests, and proposals for early commercial applications.

Of growing importance are alliances with other entities, especially cable companies, as emphasized in Chapter 1. Strong synergies exist between the telephone and cable industries (in contrast, say, to television broadcasting). The LECs have long experience in building dependable, two-way wireline networks. Their total lack of experience in supplying residential video is exactly the ingredient that cable operators can offer. Consequently, it should come as no surprise to see the recent negotiations between telephone companies and MSOs.

Telephone companies gain in two ways. First, access to the cable systems of the partner MSO will facilitate their participation in out-of-territory video (as well as telephone) services. By the same token, the MSO can draw from expertise of its out-of-territory telephone partner to facilitate entry into telephone markets in territories served by its cable systems. As Raymond Smith, Chairman and Chief Executive Officer of Bell Atlantic said shortly after the announcement of his

---

54. For an informative account of the business pressures faced by the LECs, see DONALDSON, LUFKIN & JENRETTE, COMPETITION IS EMERGING IN THE U.S. TELEPHONE MARKET (June 7, 1991).

55. NATIONAL CABLE TELEVISION ASS'N, *supra* note 8.

company's plan to acquire TCI, "We can take our expertise into TCI, and we can save these people five years. We know every blind alley there is."[56] The planned merger later was abandoned, but not ostensibly on the grounds that Bell Atlantic and TCI had misjudged the potential synergies from combining their firms.

Second, in alliance with a cable MSO, the LEC will be better able to provide in-territory video. At the same time, since they will face stronger cable incumbents, who also benefit from alliances with telephone companies, the LECs may be in no better position, on balance, to compete with the cable incumbents than described above.

Issues immediately arise about whether such alliances tend to be procompetitive or anticompetitive and, more generally, what public policies should be adopted to help ensure socially desirable outcomes. These issues are treated in Chapter 5.

Conclusions

Despite the widespread interest in the potential of fiber for video services provided by the LECs, they will face great difficulty in competing with incumbent cable operators (including out-of-territory telephone companies), at least during the remainder of this decade. Widespread in-territory competition can be expected only if the LECs find some way to use their existing copper networks for satisfactory video transmission or if consumer demand for channel capacity is so large that both the LECs and cable operators would be obliged to build wholly new networks.

For three reasons, we must be cautious about the prospects for mushrooming new service markets in response to the construction of fiber networks. First, many commonly mentioned new services could be supplied with combinations of today's telephone and cable networks. The stumbling block lies not in the absence of fiber but in a sufficient consumer demand to offset the high cost of software development. Second, no resounding successes have yet been reported from the numerous experiments and field trials in recent years. Third, many new

---

56. BROADCASTING & CABLE, Nov. 8, 1993, at 20.

services will be partial substitutes among themselves and with existing services. A strong demand for one will be, in part at least, at the expense of others.

Despite this less-than-upbeat appraisal of the LECs' prospects in video, strong reasons exist for them to seek out opportunities, as they are now doing with their plans for broadband networks as one component in a diversified portfolio of business activities. If the experience proves unfavorable during the next few years, these plans can be modified or even canceled. In the meantime, the LECs' parent telephone companies may do well in out-of-territory video markets, in partnerships, or in mergers with cable MSOs.

4

Video Dialtone and
Local Telephone Companies

ALTHOUGH WE CONCLUDED in Chapter 3 that the LECs face a tough struggle in competing with incumbent cable operators, at least during this decade, it surely does not follow that the LECs should be prohibited from trying. Rather, the challenge is to design appropriate legislative and regulatory ground rules for LEC participation in the video marketplace.

To facilitate assessment of technological and economic factors, we assumed in Chapter 3 that the LECs have the same freedom of action in the video marketplace as cable operators do. It is time to relax this assumption. As a matter of public policy, the LECs are severely constrained in their ability to participate. Under terms of the cross-ownership ban, they are not permitted to offer video service directly to the public within their telephone operating territories. As common carriers, unlike cable operators, they are permitted to provide video only under terms of nondiscriminatory access to potential program suppliers with no LEC control over content. Moreover, the Bell Operating Companies (BOCs) are prohibited from carrying video signals across LATA boundaries, thereby limiting their contiguous geographical coverage.[1] These constraints are imposed because of widely voiced concerns that the LECs would otherwise subsidize their video activities at the expense of their telephone ratepayers and engage in anticompetitive practices through control of their bottleneck transmission facilities.

In contrast, cable operators are free, with limited exceptions, to

1. *See infra* note 73 and accompanying text.

discriminate among program suppliers and to control content. They are regarded as electronic publishers for which, like newspaper publishers, the functions of programming, editing, and distribution are combined. Some are vertically integrated into program supply; that is, they hold ownership interests in cable program networks, as discussed below.[2]

This chapter focuses on policy issues arising from the constraints faced by the LECs in participating in the video marketplace. First, it traces the evolution of public policy, including the FCC's decision to permit the LECs to offer video dialtone, and current legislative and judicial moves to lift the cross-ownership ban. Second, it evaluates the common-carrier obligations embodied in video dialtone as an impediment to LEC competition with cable operators. Third, it calls into question the economic viability of video dialtone in a market populated by cable incumbents. Fourth, it explores how the failure to achieve common-carrier video transmission would affect information diversity. Fifth, it describes the nature of cross-subsidization and addresses the adequacy of current safeguards. Finally, it examines the prohibition on interLATA video transmission by the Bell companies.

The Evolution of Public Policy

Because cable operators have been heavily dependent on access to LEC poles and conduits, cable's early history was marked by conflicts with the LECs about the terms for access to these bottleneck facilities. Even without video competition between the two entities, allegations abounded about price gouging and other unfair LEC practices. Were LECs to enter the video market, many argued, they would have even greater incentive to engage in anticompetitive behavior.

In response, in 1970 the FCC imposed cross-ownership rules—later codified in the Cable Act of 1984—that generally barred the LECs from entering the cable television industry. Section 63.54 of the FCC's rules implementing the Communications Act of 1934 provides:

No telephone common carrier subject in whole or in part to the Communications Act of 1934 shall engage in the provision of video

---

2. To be sure, cable operators do not have complete control over content: they carry signals of local broadcasting stations whose content they do not control. Moreover, cable operators are subject to leased-access requirements and to other access requirements specified in the Cable Acts of 1984 and 1992, as discussed below.

programming to the viewing public in its telephone service area, either directly, or indirectly through an affiliate owned by, operated by, controlled by, or under common control with the telephone common carrier.[3]

LEC participation was limited to offering leased channels under common-carrier arrangements, called channel service, to cable operators duly franchised by the cognizant local authority, as stipulated under section 214 of the 1934 Act.[4]

Subsequent developments brought pressures for regulatory change. The hammering out of more or less satisfactory arrangements between LECs and cable operators for rights to poles and conduits—combined with federal and state legislation—has mitigated the problem of cable access. Most notably, in 1978 Congress passed the Pole Attachment Act, which authorized the Commission to "regulate the rates, terms, and conditions for pole attachments."[5] Moreover, large subscriber rate increases after passage of the 1984 Cable Act stimulated the search for public policies to promote competition. The potential of fiber technology encouraged the notion that the LECs would be particularly good candidates for competitive entry.

Consequently, in 1988 the FCC tentatively concluded that the cross-ownership ban should be lifted.[6] Addressing the competitive consequences of lifting the ban, the Commission reasoned:

On the one hand, where independent cable service is available, . . . entry by telephone companies would seem to bring all the benefits generally associated with competition, including greater choice for consumers, greater innovation, lower prices, and greater responsiveness to consumer demand. On the other hand, where independent cable service does not now exist, telephone company entry

---

3. 47 C.F.R. § 63.54(a). This prohibition is subject to waiver, in accordance with specified criteria, in sparsely populated areas. *See* 47 U.S.C. § 533(b).

4. *Id.* § 214(a).

5. *Id.* § 224(b)(1). Although this Act is addressed to fears of discriminatory pricing for pole attachments, it is applicable only if access is actually granted by the LEC. The LEC can avoid being subject to provisions of the Act by simply refusing to grant access.

6. Telephone Company-Cable Television Cross-Ownership Rules, Sections 63.54-63.58, Further Notice of Inquiry and Notice of Proposed Rulemaking, CC Dkt. No. 87-266, 3 F.C.C. Rcd. 5849, 5851 ¶ 10 (1988).

would bring new services to areas previously unserved.[7]

Because the cross-ownership ban was codified in the 1984 Cable Act, however, congressional rather than FCC action would be required to modify or rescind the ban. Amid continuing controversy, the Commission made no final decision in 1988 to recommend to Congress that the cross-ownership ban be lifted.

In 1992, the Commission decided to permit the LECs to offer to "multiple service providers on a nondiscriminatory common carrier basis, a basic platform that will deliver video programming and other services to end users."[8] For this service, called video dialtone, LECs are not to control the content of programming or to make decisions about "the price, terms, and conditions of video programming offered to consumers."[9] This decision reflected the Commission's desire to advance its "overarching goals of creating opportunities to develop an advanced telecommunications infrastructure, increasing competition in the video marketplace, and enhancing the diversity of video services to the American public."[10]

Three characteristics of the FCC's interpretation of video dialtone are especially notable. First, video dialtone may be offered by LECs without video service being provided directly to subscribers "in the manner of traditional cable operators." Therefore, implementation of video dialtone requires not revision of the Cable Act, but only revision of those portions of the FCC's cross-ownership rules that were *not* codified in the Act.[11]

Second, the Commission concluded that the provisions of the Cable Act do not require that the LEC or programmers using its network obtain a local cable television franchise to offer video dialtone, because the Commission interprets video common carriage as not being a "cable television service" as defined by the Act.[12] Whether video

7. *Id.* at 5873 n.49.

8. Telephone Company-Cable Television Rules, Sections 63.54-63.58, Second Report and Order, Recommendation to Congress, and Second Further Notice of Proposed Rulemaking, CC Dkt. No, 87-266, 7 F.C.C. Rcd. 5781, 5783 ¶ 2 (1992) [hereinafter *Video Dialtone Order*].

9. *Id.* at 5789 ¶ 14.

10. *Id.* at 5783 ¶ 1.

11. *Id.* at 5789 ¶ 14.

12. *Id.* at 5806-08 ¶¶ 47-52.

dialtone is a permissible offering without revision of the Act or whether providers of video dialtone are free of local franchise requirements is subject to debate and courtroom appeals. We do not deal with the legal issues in this study but assume, for purposes of economic and technical analysis, that the Commission's actions withstand legal challenge.

Third, despite the widespread enthusiasm for fiber as noted earlier, the Commission has declined to support explicitly the use of fiber or any other specific technology.

> It is not our intent, nor our proper role, to specify the technology, network architecture, or functions that a telephone company would offer under video dialtone. Given the rapid pace of technological development in this area, our policy initially sets only the necessary broad regulatory framework and relies upon the technical and market creativity of those in the private sector responding to market demand and economics to determine the substance of telephone company video dialtone offerings.[13]

This stance reflects the recognition of that, in addition to fiber, other ways may emerge to provide video—including the upgrading of existing copper networks for broadband use—as emphasized in Chapter 3.

Although the LECs generally agree that video dialtone is a step in the right direction, they have argued that its common-carrier constraints are overly burdensome. Among others, Bell Atlantic has asserted, "If consumers are to reap the benefits of true competition, telephone companies must be permitted to compete in both the transport and creation of video programming."[14]

The Commission, too, was persuaded that the public interest would be served if the LECs were permitted to go beyond video dialtone:

> Although we find that the ability of local telephone companies to offer video dialtone will improve competition in the video market, we also agree that under video dialtone, local telephone companies will not be on an equal footing with cable companies because they

---

13. *Id.* at 5788 ¶ 13.

14. Harry A. Jessell, *Video Dialtone Falls Short for Telcos*, BROADCASTING, Feb. 10, 1992, at 48. This account is a good summary of the reactions of LECs to the limitations imposed on them by video dialtone.

will be limited in the range of services they can offer in response to market demand. Moreover, we conclude that the ability of local telephone companies to have significant ownership interests in video programmers, particularly independent and start-up services, will further increase competition in the video market.[15]

Consequently, at the time of its video dialtone decision, the Commission recommended to Congress that the 1984 Cable Act be amended to permit LECs greater freedom, going beyond video dialtone, to compete with cable operators and other multichannel suppliers by exercising control over programming "subject to appropriate safeguards."[16]

Thus, the future of the ban depends on congressional and judicial action. During 1993, bills were introduced in both the House and Senate to lift the ban.[17] Passage of legislation is anticipated in many quarters during 1994.

In December 1992, Bell Atlantic brought action in the U.S. District Court in Alexandria, Virginia, challenging the ban on First Amendment and other constitutional grounds. In August 1993, the court ruled that the ban is unconstitutional both on its face and as applied to the plaintiff's particular circumstances.[18]

The court's decision, however, does not lift the ban nationwide. In mid-1993, the court affirmed that its decision pertains only to Bell Atlantic's telephone operating territory of six states and the District of Columbia. Other telephone companies seeking relief are obliged to bring suit for relief in their own territories. By early 1994, all the RBOCs had filed court suits,[19] while the Department of Justice was appealing the Bell Atlantic decision in the U.S. Court of Appeals for

---

15. *Video Dialtone Order, supra* note 8, at 5850 ¶ 140. Of course, if the LEC were allowed to deal directly with subscribers, through modification of the Cable Act, it would still be obliged to obtain a local cable franchise unless other federal action were taken to preempt local authority.

16. *Id.* at 5784 ¶ 3.

17. *See* S. 1086, 103d Cong., 1st Sess. (1993) (Telecommunications Infrastructure Act of 1993); H.R. 1504, 103d Cong., 1st Sess. (1993) (Communications Competitiveness and Infrastructure Modernization Act of 1993); H.R. 3636, 103d Cong., 1st Sess. (1993) (National Communications Competition and Information Infrastructure Act of 1993).

18. Chesapeake & Potomac Tel. Co. of Va. *v.* United States, 830 F. Supp. 909 (E.D. Va. 1993).

19. TELECOMMUNICATIONS REP., Feb. 7, 1994, at 21.

the Fourth Circuit. It is easy to anticipate the case going as far as the Supreme Court, probably in 1994 or 1995.

Common-Carrier Obligations

Of major importance are the consequences of common-carrier obligations imposed on LECs, in accordance with the FCC's video dialtone decision, while cable operators remain free of such burden. Focusing on common carriage is important because (1) concerns about common-carriage obligations have played a prominent role in the history of cable,[20] (2) LEC entry into video is predicated on the concept of a common-carrier–based video dialtone, and (3) even if the cross-ownership ban is lifted, the LECs may remain subject to common-carrier requirements, as discussed in Chapter 5.

To proceed, we must first clarify the concept of common carriage.[21] The Communications Act of 1934 specifies that each carrier must (1) "furnish . . . communication service upon reasonable request"[22] and (2) file a schedule "showing all charges for itself and its connecting carriers."[23] Especially relevant for our purposes, the Act stipulates:

It shall be unlawful for any common carrier to make any unjust or unreasonable discrimination in charges, practices, classifications, regulations, facilities, or services for or in connection with like communication service, directly or indirectly, by any means or device, or to make or give any undue or unreasonable preference or advantage to any particular person, class of persons, or locality, or to subject any particular person, class of persons, or locality to any undue or unreasonable prejudice or disadvantage.[24]

Of key importance is what does and does not constitute an "undue or unreasonable preference." In fact, the courts and regulators have

20. The following discussion of concerns about public access draws from STANLEY M. BESEN & LELAND L. JOHNSON, AN ECONOMIC ANALYSIS OF MANDATORY LEASED CHANNEL ACCESS FOR CABLE TELEVISION (RAND 1982).

21. For a detailed treatment, see MICHAEL K. KELLOGG, JOHN THORNE & PETER W. HUBER, FEDERAL TELECOMMUNICATIONS LAW 112-18 (Little, Brown & Co. 1992).

22. 47 U.S.C. § 201(a).

23. *Id.* § 203.

24. *Id.* § 202(a).

permitted telephone companies rather wide leeway in charging different rates among classes of users (for example, residential and small business users) even when the costs of service are the same: "[P]rice discrimination remains the norm rather than the exception across the telephone industry."[25]

The distinction between common carriage and non-common carriage is one of degree, hinging on how broadly classes of customers are defined. At one extreme is the carrier that charges the same rate to *all* customers for whom the cost of service is the same. In practice, no carrier conforms to such an extreme degree of nondiscrimination. Next, some carriers charge different rates for various customer classes (with the same underlying costs), but with each class defined rather broadly. Thus, discrimination is judged not unreasonable between residential and small business telephone users. But the firm, as a common carrier, would be in trouble if it proposed varied rate structures for residential service based, say, on family size. Finally, we can imagine other carriers engaging in *perfect* price discrimination. Like common carriers, they would charge different rates to different customer classes. But customer classes would be defined so narrowly that only a single customer would fit within each class.

From these comparisons, we can anticipate that, with video dialtone, the LEC will be permitted to offer network access rates that differ among broad classes of users, such as between advertiser-supported video and that supported by the Corporation for Public Broadcasting. But it would have difficulty justifying differences in access rates, say, among packagers of popular movies. In contrast, cable operators are quite free to engage in such discrimination.

The Nonviability of Video Dialtone?

The analysis in Chapter 3 suggests that the LECs would have great difficulty competing with incumbent cable operators even if they were on a full parity with respect to carriage obligations and restrictions. The imposition of common-carriage video dialtone requirements on the LECs will make competition even more difficult. To be sure, the exemption of the LECs and their programmer-customers from local franchise requirements, which the FCC concludes would be permissible

---

25. KELLOGG, THORNE & HUBER, *supra* note 21, at 117.

under the 1984 Cable Act, would confer some offsetting benefit. Even so, the LECs would face severe difficulties in discharging common-carrier obligations as delineated in the Commission's video dialtone decision.

The root consideration is that LEC video networks would be operated more profitably as cable networks are today rather than as common carriers. The freedom of cable operators to discriminate is well described by the National Cable Television Association:

In assembling [program] packages, operators virtually never negotiate identical terms and prices for all program services. Operators pay different amounts for different services, and these differences are based on the different operating costs of such services, the different demand for such services among consumers, and the different value that each service brings to the tier or package of services provided by the operator.[26]

The greater profitability afforded by discriminatory treatment underlies the strong opposition that cable operators have repeatedly voiced to the imposition of common-carrier obligations on themselves.

In 1972, the FCC ruled that cable operators must make available a limited number of channels for lease by others.[27] In the late 1970s, however, the FCC's jurisdiction over cable was challenged, and the Supreme Court struck down the FCC's access requirement because it cast cable systems in the role of common carriers.[28] The Court held that because the Communications Act of 1934 explicitly prohibits the FCC from treating broadcasters as common carriers, and because the FCC's authority with respect to cable was based on its jurisdiction over broadcasting, no common-carrier requirement could legally be imposed on cable by the Commission.

In addition to court challenges that led to the overturning of the FCC's cable access requirements in the late 1970s, opposition by the cable industry led to weakened access requirements in the 1984 Cable Act. The Act requires that cable systems with specified characteristics make available channels for commercial lease by unaffiliated entities.

26. National Cable Television Ass'n, Comments, MM Dkt. No. 92-266, at 91 (Jan. 27, 1993).

27. 47 C.F.R. § 76.254(a)(4).

28. FCC *v.* Midwest Video Corp., 440 U.S. 689 (1979).

The purpose is "to assure that the widest possible diversity of information sources is made available to the public from cable systems in a manner consistent with growth and development of cable systems."[29] The requirement does not apply to systems with fewer than thirty-six activated channels. Systems with thirty-six to fifty-four activated channels must set aside 10 percent for leased access, and those with more than fifty-four activated channels must set aside 15 percent.[30]

For four reasons, these access requirements have been largely ineffective. First, cable operators have been free to establish lease rates and other conditions such that leased access "will not adversely affect the operation, financial condition, or market development of the cable system."[31] Subject to such general constraints, cable operators have the latitude to reject programming.

Second, cable operators have not been required to provide "marketing, billing, or other such services"[32] to channel lessees. Costs could be high for such activities conducted channel by channel. In principle, lessees could cooperate in sharing the costs of marketing and billing. But joint action is handicapped because the maximum number of access channels is low. A forty-channel system, for example, is obliged to offer no more than four leased channels.

Third, the enforcement mechanism has been cumbersome. Aggrieved parties may resort to the federal courts and to the FCC, but with a heavy burden of proof on themselves. The courts and the FCC are "directed to presume" that the price and conditions of access in question are "reasonable and in good faith unless shown by clear and convincing evidence to the contrary."[33]

Fourth, cable operators have not been required under the 1984 Act to offer nondiscriminatory access as a common carrier. They are permitted to consider the "nature (but not the specific editorial content)

29. 47 U.S.C. § 532(a).

30. *Id.* § 532(b). The 1984 Cable Act also permits local franchising authorities to require cable systems to set aside channels for public, educational, and government use (so-called PEG channels).

31. Competition, Rate Deregulation and the Commission's Policies Relating to the Provision of Cable Television Service, Report, MM Dkt. No. 89-600, 5 F.C.C. Rcd. 4962, 5046 ¶ 171 (1990) [hereinafter *1990 Cable Report*].

32. *Id.* at 5047 ¶ 173.

33. *Id.* at 5048 ¶ 175.

of the service . . . , how it will affect the marketing of the mix of existing services being offered by the cable operator to subscribers, as well as potential market fragmentation that might be created."[34]

Recognizing the weaknesses of the provisions for commercial leased access in the 1984 Act, Congress added provisions to the 1992 Act to give the Commission expanded authority to determine the maximum reasonable rates and terms of use that a cable operator may establish for leased channels, including rates for billing and revenue collection, and to establish procedures for expediting resolution of disputes.[35]

In May 1993, the Commission addressed the issue of setting reasonable rates only by specifying that "in the rules adopted we set a standard for charging maximum leased access rates based on the *highest* implicit fee charged any nonaffiliated programmer within the same program category."[36] It also established a procedure for expediting the resolution of disputes.

The basic structure of the leased-access rules set down in the 1984 Cable Act, however, remains intact. As the National Cable Television Association emphasizes, the 1992 Cable Act

> does not seek to eliminate the cable operator's function of selecting and packaging programming for sale to subscribers and to instead require systems to operate in a leased access mode. To the contrary, Congress intended to preserve the traditional editorial and packaging functions of cable operators, while crafting a leased access mechanism that could *co-exist* with those functions.[37]

With cable operators retaining their non-common-carrier status under the most recent legislation while common-carrier obligations are imposed on the LECs' provision of video dialtone, we explore how the asymmetry in carrier treatment of cable and LEC-supplied video is likely to affect the prospects for competition between them. To do so,

---

34. *Id.* at 5047 ¶ 173.

35. 47 U.S.C. § 532(c)(4)(A).

36. Implementation of Sections of the Cable Television Consumer Protection and Competition Act of 1992, Rate Regulation, Report and Order, and Further Notice of Proposed Rulemaking, MM Dkt. 92-266, 8 F.C.C. Rcd. 5631, 5936 ¶ 492 (1993) (emphasis added).

37. National Cable Television Ass'n, Comments, MM Dkt. No. 92-266, at 89 (Jan. 27, 1993).

let us assume that either ADSL is satisfactorily developed for LEC use or that fiber-based systems give the LECs a stronger competitive advantage than was depicted in Chapter 3. Under these circumstances, consider the outcome of a LEC's deploying a video-dialtone network that would make available—as the FCC describes it—to "multiple service providers on a non-discriminatory common carrier basis, a basic platform that will deliver video programming and other services to end users."[38]

With the LEC platform in place, we could not expect service providers to go door to door with single-channel offerings—especially since the incumbent cable operator would already have signed up (with converters and other equipment in place) perhaps 60 percent of the homes. More probably, LECs would enter into multichannel marketing agreements with service providers to offer bundles of programs to the subscriber—not unlike the tiers of programming offered by cable operators. Indeed, with the economies of consolidated marketing, a single dominant service provider might emerge to offer various combinations of tiers, pay-per-view programming, and other services. If so, the dominant service provider would resemble today's cable operator—with a leased-access fringe to accommodate others. The major difference is that the physical network would be leased, rather than owned, by the service provider. In this case, the common-carrier objectives of video dialtone would not be achieved.

The role of local franchising is also relevant. The one advantage to participants in the preceding example is freedom from local franchising (if the Commission's interpretation of the 1984 Cable Act is upheld in court). Suppose, in contrast, the decision is not upheld, thereby negating this advantage. Since a franchise would be required in any event, LECs might be tempted simply to lease their networks directly to incumbent cable operators as a section 214 channel service. Doing so would mitigate the delays and uncertainties of holding out their networks to all comers; it would also assure incumbent cable operators of access to LEC networks under sufficiently attractive terms to make channel service a favorable alternative to upgrading existing cable systems. Again, the common-carrier objectives of video dialtone would not be achieved.

In conclusion, we must entertain the possibility that video dialtone will be a nonviable, transitory concept. In whatever way LECs seek to

38. *Video Dialtone Order, supra* note 8, at 5783 ¶ 2.

enter the video market, the outcome may resemble that of the cable model rather than the one envisioned today for video dialtone.

How would failure to attain the FCC's common-carrier goals affect social welfare? The answer, perhaps surprisingly, is that this outcome might not make much difference to society. The reasons, to which we now turn, are that (1) it is not necessarily true that common carriage would increase programming diversity and (2) expanded capacity made available by advanced networks will encourage greater diversity with or without common-carriage obligations.

Effects on Information Diversity

Information diversity has three dimensions: (1) the number of information sources, (2) the differences among them, and (3) the terms under which they are made available to potential users.[39] To illustrate, if two television programs have identical content and are offered under identical conditions to viewers, diversity is not increased by including the second offering. At the other extreme, if the information content of the two is wholly dissimilar, the availability of both would increase diversity. In the middle is the commonly observed case of programs with some degree of similarity (for example, two newscasts with differing slants on the news).

The terms of program availability involve three components: (1) convenience, (2) price, and (3) geographical location. With respect to the first, a television program offered only at 2:00 A.M. would contribute less to diversity than if it were offered during prime time. Conversely, if the program were offered both during prime time and at 2:00 A.M., availability—and information diversity—would be broadened. With respect to price, a given program may contribute to diversity in terms of content, but the price to potential users might be so high that only a few are willing to pay. Thus, a channel of programs priced at $10 per month would contribute less to diversity than if the price were $5. Finally, with respect to geographical availability, a program shown only on the East Coast contributes less to diversity than would be true with nationwide coverage.

Common carriage has three advantages in terms of information diversity. First, some programs not carried by the non-common carrier

39. LELAND L. JOHNSON, COMMON CARRIER VIDEO DELIVERY BY TELEPHONE COMPANIES 17 (RAND 1992).

because of their adverse effect on the revenues of other programs would be carried by the common carrier.

Second, the common carrier's published tariffs would give program suppliers greater certainty about the costs they would face to reach the viewing public. In contrast, access by the non–common carrier is subject to negotiation and attendant uncertainty about the geographical coverage that program suppliers would be able to achieve. Less uncertainty about access would encourage the production of programming that otherwise would not appear.

Third, for some program suppliers, charges for access to the common carrier network would be lower than otherwise. Those who paid relatively high rates under discriminatory access would see their access changes fall under the rules of common carriage.

A potential *disadvantage* of common carriage, however, is that some program suppliers would be unable to pay a nondiscriminatory access charge even though they would be able to pay a lower fee sufficient to cover the incremental cost incurred by the common carrier in providing access. The non–common carrier, free to discriminate, would more likely carry this programming.

On balance, we cannot conclude that common carriage would be superior to unconstrained carriage on the grounds of information diversity, because it is impossible to quantify and weigh the preceding conflicting factors. Let us assume, however, that common carriage *would* add to information diversity; that is, the first three factors above outweigh the fourth. What is the value of the additional social benefits from the additional diversity? We ask this question because information diversity, presumably like other goods and services, is subject to diminishing returns. Although expanded diversity has a positive value to society, the value of an *increment* of diversity falls as the level expands. Thus, for two otherwise identical societies, an increase in diversity in one society with an existing abundance would be valued less than the same increase in the other society with little diversity.

To probe further, let us consider diversity in units that can be added together to enable society to place a value on each increment or unit added. In Table 4–1, six increments of diversity of one unit each are listed on the left. The social value of each increment reflects the fact that the value of each additional unit falls as the number increases; that is, information diversity is subject to diminishing returns. Thus, society values the first increment at $25 but the sixth increment at only $2.

TABLE 4–1
VALUE OF DIVERSITY AND VIDEO CARRIAGE ON
ALTERNATIVE NETWORKS

		Carriage of Units of Diversity			
		Today's Network		Advanced Network	
Units of Diversity	Value of Each Increment ($)	Common Carrier	Non-Common Carrier	Common Carrier	Non-Common Carrier
1	25	1	1	1	1
1	20	1	1	1	1
1	15	1		1	1
1	10			1	1
1	5			1	
1	2			1	

SOURCE: JOHNSON, *supra* note 39, at 65.

Consider two video networks, today's network incorporating current technology and an advanced network incorporating expanded use of fiber alone with video compression, without reference to whether the facilities are owned by LECs or cable companies. The use of advanced technologies permits cost reductions so that, with other factors held constant, more channels are used than with today's network. With today's network, the common carrier produces three units of diversity compared with only two units for the non–common carrier. The social value of common carriage, which is the value of the additional diversity produced, is equal to $15—the value of the third unit that otherwise would not be produced. With the advanced network, the carrier produces six units of diversity as a common carrier but only four units as a non–common carrier. Thus, common carriage in the advanced network calls forth a greater increase in diversity (two units) than it does in today's network (one unit). Society, however, values this increase at only $7 (the total for the last two increments), compared with $15 for the increase of one increment produced today.

This outcome suggests that a common–carriage requirement will become progressively less important as upgraded or new video networks are built. The expansion of network capacity, with or without common–carrier obligations, will enable an expansion of information diversity. The social value of the additional diversity that would have been afforded by common carriage will fall as channel capacity expands.

Moreover, additional competition in the video market will reduce the importance of common carriage. Although widespread two-wire video competition is unlikely, at least during this decade, competition may well emerge from wireless technologies, as discussed later. Competing networks will contribute to information diversity, even though none operates as a common carrier.

The Threat of Cross-Subsidization

To this point, we have focused on basic technical and economic considerations to conclude that the prospects are questionable for the LECs, by upgrading their networks, to compete with incumbent cable operators. This conclusion, however, reflects no consideration of whether cross-subsidization would affect outcomes. Would the LECs subsidize video dialtone by shifting video costs to their monopoly telephone ratepayers? If so, would they not proceed to enter the video market, in competition with cable operators, even if the underlying economies are unfavorable? The threat of cross-subsidization poses the most difficult of all the problems treated in this monograph.

Cross-Subsidy and Incremental Costs. To proceed, we first must define cross-subsidy. We do so under the assumption that, in all cases, the regulated firm just covers its costs, including only a normal profit. For two services, X and Y, cross-subsidy exists if the incremental revenue from X is insufficient to cover the incremental cost of X, but the firm nevertheless earns sufficient revenues from Y to cover the investment and all other outlays for X and Y together.[40] The incremental cost of X is defined as the difference between the firm's total cost with and without service X. Thus, if cross-subsidy exists, users of Y pay more for Y if the firm simultaneously provides X than they would in the absence of X, because revenues for X are insufficient to cover the additional (or incremental) costs that it imposes on the firm. Here, we can conveniently think of Y as being telephone service and X as being video service. Cross-subsidy would not arise so long as each service, telephone and video, covers at least its incremental cost. In that event, telephone users would pay no more if the LEC also provides video service than in the absence of video. Indeed, if video revenues were to exceed video's incremental cost, telephone ratepayers would stand to benefit from the joint supply of the two services.

The danger of cross-subsidy is of special concern for the firm that is regulated through the traditional rate-of-return approach, where its prices are controlled by a ceiling on its profits:

Observers have often argued that the incentive for such cross-subsidies is enhanced by profit-ceiling regulation, for the profit ceiling provides the firm with a pool of unused potential profits that, in the absence of cross-subsidy, regulation does not permit it to exploit fully. If so, the firm can perhaps accept losses on its competitive services with greater equanimity, pricing those services at levels that make sense only as means to harm competitors. For the regulated firm can make up for those losses out of its untapped profits, if clever accounting and legal arguments can persuade the regulator to permit this on the grounds that earnings will otherwise be inadequate.[41]

If intent on cross-subsidizing, the LEC would seek to overestimate the incremental cost of telephone service and to underestimate the incremental cost of video service. To detect cross-subsidy, then, regulators must estimate accurately the incremental cost of the service in question.

The task of protecting against cross-subsidization would be easy if each expenditure incurred by the LEC could be uniquely identified with either telephone or video service. Unfortunately, complications arise when the services are offered on the same network. To illustrate, consider an electronics package required to transmit and to manipulate the signals passing through the fiber cables. Suppose that the cost of the package is $100 per home for telephone and video offered jointly, $60 if the electronics are supplied only for telephone, and $90 if sup-

41. *Id.* at 85.

plied only for video. Thus, the incremental cost is $10 for telephone and $40 for video. So long as video subscribers pay no less than $40, telephone subscribers would pay no more than $60—no more than they would be obliged to pay without video. Thus, cross-subsidization of video would not arise. Expressed differently, so long as telephone subscribers pay no more than $60, which is their stand-alone or separate network cost, they would not be burdened by the presence of video and, hence, would not subsidize video.

The challenge for the regulator is to discover the true incremental costs—a task complicated by the fact that the LEC knows much more than the regulator does about network design and operation. Suppose that the LEC reports to the regulator that the incremental cost of video is only $15 (instead of $40) and that $30 in video revenues can be expected. If the revenue projections are borne out, a subsidy of $10 will flow to video subscribers from telephone ratepayers, who will be burdened with a payment of $70, or $10 more than their $60 stand-alone cost.

To identify the true incremental cost hinges on knowing the cost of the electronics if only telephone and, alternatively, if only video were provided. The nub of the problem is that cases may not exist where the particular package of electronics in question *is* used for only one or the other. The LEC and the regulator might find themselves in seemingly endless disagreement about what the electronics would have cost in a hypothetical world in which the two services would be offered singly.

The situation is further complicated by the possibility that a network optimally designed only for telephony might not need this electronics package at all. The optimal network for telephony alone (for example, a digital loop carrier) may be quite different from the one for integrated service. Disputes about design and cost of such a telephone network would be complicated by the fact that the network would be hypothetical, rather than one being proposed by the LEC.

Finally, complications arise because the LEC is not starting from a clean slate. Throughout our discussion, we have examined alternative network designs as if they were planned for new communities in which all telecommunication facilities are yet to be built. In contrast, the great bulk of LEC fiber construction is planned in areas that already have telephone service, as well as cable. The analyst must consider not only the incremental cost of adding telephony to a proposed integrated network but also the cost of simply upgrading the existing stand-alone network for continued telephone service as an alternative to the telephone portion of the integrated network. If the cost of the upgrade is lower than the telephone portion of a new integrated network, the upgrade cost becomes the relevant measure for identifying the presence of cross-subsidy.

This point is extremely important. To install fiber to the neighborhood or to the curb for integrated service will require that the LECs essentially scrap their existing copper networks. Evaluation of a network upgrade, as a substitute for wholly new construction, could make an enormous difference.

To illustrate, consider $1,400 per subscriber as the cost of a fiber network for video alone, $1,650 for video and telephone jointly, and $800 for telephone alone. Suppose further that everyone agrees that these are the true costs. Thus, as long as video subscribers pay no less than the incremental cost of $850 ($1,650 – $800), they will not be subsidized by telephone subscribers. Suppose, however, that only $100 is required to upgrade and to maintain the existing copper network for whatever telephone services would have been offered on the proposed fiber network. In this case, telephone users should pay no more than $100, which is their stand-alone cost. To avoid cross-subsidy, video subscribers would have to pay no less than $1,550, rather than a minimum of $850. If video subscribers pay only $850, telephone subscribers will have to cover $800, which is far more than their $100 stand-alone cost. Given these numbers, video users would also be better off with a dedicated video network in the absence of subsidy, for which they would pay only $1,400 instead of $1,550.

In short, regulators will face an unenviable task in evaluating the LEC's estimates. Not only must these figures be assessed as they stand, but regulators must go beyond them to consider "what-if" scenarios for providing the services being proposed by the LECs. Especially, regulators must be cautious when LECs propose scrapping existing copper networks (which generally work quite well for telephone services) and replacing them with integrated fiber facilities.

In all this, the danger is not so much that the LECs will premeditatedly commit to plans that involve some expected billions of dollars in subsidies from telephone ratepayers. Rather, the danger is that they will embark on riskier ventures than otherwise, knowing that, if worst comes to worst, they can count on telephone ratepayers for bailout. If optimistic market forecasts and cost estimates materialize, all may turn out well. Otherwise, telephone ratepayers stand to lose with the LEC able to compete at below cost against cable operators and other multichannel providers.

In light of the pervasive economic and technological uncertainties and ambiguities in the kinds of cost analysis illustrated above, the LECs have ample leeway to fool the regulators if they are intent on cross-subsidizing. The key issue relates to the adequacy of existing regulatory safeguards and changing market structures that affect the *ability* of the LECs to cross-subsidize.

The FCC's View. Potential LEC entry into video is just the latest example where concerns about cross-subsidization have emerged in the telephone industry. The Commission has grappled with the problem throughout the history of telephone company involvement in competitive markets and has established a number of protective measures. In its video dialtone decision, the Commission concluded that "existing safeguards against discrimination and cross-subsidization . . . should protect against potential anticompetitive conduct by local telephone companies providing video dialtone."[42] The Commission emphasized that "we intend to reassess the adequacy of our existing safeguards at such time as local telephone companies present us with specific video dialtone proposals in connection with a Section 214 authorization certificate."[43] It concluded that "any remaining risk of anticompetitive conduct . . . is outweighed by the potential public interest benefits, especially regarding the quantity and diversity of video programming produced."[44]

Accounting Rules. Among the Commission's regulatory safeguards, accounting rules are the most important. By delineating the procedures to be used by the firm for allocating costs among its services, these rules are intended to prevent directly the shifting of video-related costs (or costs of other competitive ventures) to monopoly ratepayers.

Costs and revenues recorded by the LECs are subject to Part 32 of the Commission's rules in the "Uniform System of Accounts for Telecommunications Companies."[45] Costs and revenues for unregulated activities are separated on the basis of each carrier's cost manual, approved in accordance with procedures adopted in the FCC's *Joint*

---

42. *Video Dialtone Order*, *supra* note 8, at 5827 ¶ 89.
43. *Id.*
44. *Id.* at 5849 ¶ 138.
45. 47 C.F.R. § 32.1-.799.

Cost Order, discussed below.[46] After all costs and revenues have been assigned to specific accounts, they are separated between the federal and state jurisdictions according to procedures in Part 36 of the Commission's rules.[47]

Unfortunately, these accounting rules provide no leeway in encouraging, or even permitting, regulators to engage in the what-if scenarios so critical to estimating incremental costs, as emphasized earlier. Accounting rules are designed to assign costs incurred to the proper accounts, not to evaluate the appropriateness of these costs in light of alternative ways the LEC might have operated. Thus, these rules provide no assurance that true incremental outlays will be identified and handled appropriately. If, for example, the carrier reports that 30 percent of the total cost of an integrated fiber network is attributable to video (instead of, say, 50 percent), regulators will face extraordinary difficulty in auditing the relevant accounts and challenging the LEC's numbers.

Common Costs. Decades of debate have gone into issues of how costs of jointly used facilities should be assigned to the services that use them. A key point of confusion in the debate is between appropriate cost allocations that forestall cross-subsidy and those seen as fair to the ratepayers in question.

As an example, consider the package of electronics noted earlier, involving a cost of $60 for telephone alone, $90 for video alone, and $100 for the two offered jointly. With a $10 incremental cost for telephone and $40 for video, how is the common cost of $50 to be allocated between the two so that the total cost of $100 is covered? As emphasized especially by economists, formulas for allocating costs lead to arbitrary, and in some cases absurd, results.[48] One such approach involves allocations in accordance with the relative use of the common facility by the services in question. As Robert Pepper points out, however, if a telephone call uses 45 Kbps and a video channel uses 45 Mbps, and if the telephone call is priced at a penny a minute (the marginal cost of an intraLATA call), then "a two-hour movie would

46. *See infra* note 55 and accompanying text.

47. *See* 47 C.F.R. § 69.1-.612.

48. For examples of how application of alternative formulas leads to arbitrary results, see William J. Baumol, Michael F. Koehn & Robert D. Willig, *How Arbitrary Is "Arbitrary"?—or, Toward the Deserved Demise of Full Cost Allocation,* PUB. UTIL. FORTNIGHTLY, Sept. 3, 1987, at 16.

cost $843.75 just for transmission."[49]

Another example, drawn from comments regarding section 214 applications for video dialtone in two areas of New Jersey,[50] illustrates a misunderstanding of what cross-subsidization involves. In response to New Jersey Bell's proposal to allocate common costs in proportion to direct investment in the two services, the Public Service Commission of the District of Columbia concluded that "since television is viewed approximately nine times as much as telephones are used, NJB's 40–50 percent [to video] allocation would appear to result in cross-subsidization of video by voice services."[51] We know from the preceding, however, that even if the proposed allocation were, say, only 10 percent, no cross-subsidization would occur so long as video covers its true incremental cost (direct investment). What the allocation does affect are the relative prices paid for video and telephone service. Thus, allocations that reduce the prices of both services in some "fair" proportion have widespread appeal. Nevertheless, all such allocations involve questions of equity, not economic efficiency.

Concentrating on economic efficiency, economists argue in favor of the Ramsey pricing rule. To cover common costs, the appropriate markup of price over marginal cost for the service in question is set inversely proportional to the price elasticity of demand for the service.[52] Thus, services with relatively inelastic demands—those whose sales are insensitive to price—would bear a large portion of common cost relative to services whose sales are sensitive to price. In this way, distortions in output caused by the need to set prices above

49. Robert M. Pepper, *Through the Looking Glass: Integrated Broadband Networks, Regulatory Policies, and Institutional Change*, 4 F.C.C. Rcd. 1306, 1313 ¶ 59 (1988).

50. New Jersey Bell, FCC Section 214 Application for Dover Township, W-P-C 6840 (Dec. 15, 1992) [hereinafter *Dover Section 214 Application*]; New Jersey Bell, Section 214 Applications for Floram Park Borough, Madison Borough, and Chatham Borough, W-P-C 6838 (Nov. 16, 1992) [hereinafter *Florham Park Section 214 Application*].

51. Public Serv. Comm'n of D.C., Comments, FCC W-P-C 6838, W-P-C 6840, at 3 (Sept. 30, 1993).

52. The price elasticity of demand is defined as the percentage change in output divided by the percentage change in price, with the result expressed as a positive number. Hence, the greater the change in output for a given change in price, the greater is the elasticity.

marginal costs are minimized.[53]

Unfortunately, the Ramsey rule is hard to apply in practice. Doing so requires accurate estimates of the elasticity of demand for the service in question. Moreover, the rule is described here under the assumption that the services are independent of each other; that is, a change in the price of one does not affect the output of the other. Frequently, however, demands are interrelated and require knowledge of cross-elasticities of demand as well and use of a more complicated Ramsey pricing rule than depicted above.[54]

Recognizing the difficulties of applying the Ramsey rule, the FCC has adopted joint-cost rules, which specify a methodology for separating the costs between the carrier's regulated and unregulated activities.[55] After the costs directly attributable to each service in question (as a proxy for incremental cost) are estimated, overhead costs (common costs) are allocated to each service in proportion to these directly attributable costs.[56]

Unlike Ramsey pricing, the Commission's approach does not require estimation of demand elasticities. But its approach leads to the Ramsey outcome only if (by sheer coincidence) the demand elasticities for the services under analysis are identical.[57]

The accounting rules help to safeguard against cross-subsidization not because their application leads to reliable estimates of incremental costs but primarily because the common cost allocated to a service provides a cushion against underestimates of incremental cost. Even if the LEC underestimates incremental costs for video, the common cost allocated to video may nevertheless assure a total above true incremental cost.

One cannot, however, safely urge large allocations of common cost to video simply as a safety margin. Protection against cross-subsidization comes at a price: the greater the level of protection, the less freedom the LEC has to compete in socially beneficial ways. Requiring particular services to cover a large portion of common cost carries the

53. For a comprehensive exposition, see William J. Baumol & David F. Bradford, *Optimal Departures from Marginal Cost Pricing*, 60 AM. ECON. REV. 265 (1970).

54. For an elaboration of the difficulties of applying Ramsey pricing, see BAUMOL & SIDAK, *supra* note 40, at 35-42.

55. Separation of Costs of Regulated Telephone Service from Costs of Nonregulated Activities, Report and Order, CC Dkt. No. 86-111, 2 F.C.C. Rcd. 1298 (1987).

56. *Id.* at 1313 ¶ 113.

57. *Id.* at 1351 n.219.

risk of encouraging uneconomic competition. Regulated carriers commonly complain of restrictions that impede their attempts to reduce rates in response to competitive pressure. If a firm is forced to maintain rates high above incremental cost, outsiders are encouraged to enter the market even though their costs are higher than the incremental costs of the incumbent.

Separate Subsidiaries. A commonly advocated requirement is that the regulated firm pursue its competitive activities only through a separate subsidiary. Several parties have urged that the Commission impose a separate-subsidiary requirement for LEC provision of enhanced gateways for video dialtone.[58] One bill considered by the 103d Congress, S. 1806, specifies that a LEC "shall not provide video programming directly to subscribers in its telephone exchange service area unless . . . such video programming is provided through a separate subsidiary . . . ."[59] Similarly, H.R. 1504 would require that such video programming be "provided through a video programming affiliate that is separate from such carrier."[60]

Such requirements are of limited help in protecting against cross-subsidization. Separation reduces the level of informal assistance that one unit of the LEC is able to give to another and reduces errors in posting charges to appropriate accounts. But it helps little with the task of identifying incremental costs. Returning to our electronic package example, a separate subsidiary requirement would not aid in determining that $40 is the true incremental cost of video. The separation requirement would help to ensure only that the $40—or whatever other figure is arrived at—is charged to the video side of the LEC'S business.

Section 214 Certification. The FCC's section 214 certification process is another regulatory safeguard intended to permit evaluation of proposed new activities in terms of public benefit. Because video dialtone is defined by the FCC as an interstate service, individual LECs must obtain section 214 certification from the FCC for proposals to offer this service. The purpose of a section 214 proceeding is well expressed by New Jersey Bell in its own applications:

---

58. *Video Dialtone Order, supra* note 8, at 5825 ¶ 83. The Commission has declined to accept this recommendation, pending the outcome of future review of the effectiveness of current safeguards. *Id.* at 5832 ¶ 96.

59. S. 1086, 103d Cong., 1st Sess., § 8 (1993).

60. H.R. 1504, 103d Cong., 1st Sess., § 652(a) (1993).

In a section 214 proceeding, the cost of the project for which authority is requested is relevant only to determine whether the cost is so substantial relative to the benefits that the public interest would not be served by construction of the project . . . . As a result, New Jersey Bell's economic justification is properly limited to showing that the direct incremental cost to add a video dial tone capability will be recovered from its projected video dial tone revenues.[61]

Accordingly, the FCC must evaluate whether the proposed venture poses a danger of cross-subsidization by examining the cost and revenue projections and other data filed by the LEC. The importance of this procedure is highlighted by the fact that, as noted earlier, the Commission is relying heavily on its experience in the section 214 process to evaluate the adequacy of its safeguards.

Effective use of the section 214 process, however, is far from straightforward. Disagreement can easily arise about whether the cost and revenue data presented by the LEC are sufficient to support well-reasoned FCC judgment. Throughout, the Commission, with far less information than the firm has, is placed in the awkward position of trying to second-guess the firm's business decisions.[62]

Incentive Regulation. Price caps and other forms of incentive regulation reduce (but do not eliminate) the threat of cross-subsidization. Focusing on control of prices rather than on rate of return and cost, the use of price caps helps to reduce perverse incentives associated with traditional rate-of-return regulation. Other incentive schemes typically involve a formal sharing of profits between the LEC and its ratepayers to strengthen its incentives to operate efficiently. States are increasingly adopting these forms of regulation.[63]

61. *Dover Section 214 Application, supra* note 50, at n.20; *Florham Park Section 214 Application, supra* note 50, at n.20.

62. For real-world examples of the difficulties of using the section 214 process for video dialtone applications, see the responses by the contending parties in the applications by New Jersey Bell, Ameritech, U S West, and Pacific Bell on file with the Commission as of February 1994. The specific information required in a section 214 application is set forth in 47 C.F.R. § 63.01.

63. For compilations of state actions, see PETER W. HUBER, MICHAEL K. KELLOGG & JOHN THORNE & THE GEODESIC NETWORK II: 1993 REPORT ON COMPETITION IN THE TELEPHONE INDUSTRY 2.51-.52 (The Geodesic Co. 1992); NATIONAL ASSOCIATION OF

These approaches to regulation reduce the ability to cross-subsidize. Telephone rate increases that would be required to support cross-subsidization may exceed the price cap—all the more so since price-cap formulas typically include a downward annual adjustment to reflect estimated productivity increases. Under profit-sharing approaches to regulation, increases in recorded telephone costs (in response to cost shifts from the subsidized sector) would result in a reduction in profits, a portion of which would affect the LEC's shareholders.

Of critcal importance, however, regulators cannot completely ignore the LEC's profits in a price-cap regime. If profits are persistently high, regulators would be under strong public pressure to revise the price-cap formula. Conversely, low profit levels or losses would bring pressure to adjust the formula in the other direction—pressures reinforced by the fact that the Fifth Amendment prohibits regulators from prescribing rates that would be confiscatory.[64]

In light of these considerations, price-cap regulation can best be regarded as a loose form of rate-of-return regulation with a formal time lag. Price-cap regimes typically include a periodic review of performance (including the historic rate of return) and an adjustment in the formula to bring the projected rate of return in line with what regulators would regard as just and reasonable.

We can imagine the regulated firm seeking to game the system by incurring excessive costs and thereby establishing a strong basis during the formal price-cap review for higher prices than otherwise. With these costs passed on to consumers (with a time lag), the firm could subsidize outside activities at the expense of its monopoly ratepayers.[65]

The process of passing costs back to the monopoly ratepayer, however, is not easy or automatic. Large proposed upward adjustments in the price-cap formula surely would be subject to scrutiny by regulators and consumer advocates. Regulators may not have a good

REGULATORY UTILITY COMMISSIONERS, THE STATUS OF COMPETITION IN INTRASTATE TELECOMMUNICATIONS 180-81 (1993).

64. *See* Louisiana Pub. Serv. Comm'n v. FCC, 476 U.S. 355, 364-65 (1986) ("[A] regulated carrier is entitled to recover its reasonable expenses and a fair return on its investment through the rates it charges its customers.").

65. *See, e.g.*, Ronald R. Braeutigam & John C. Panzar, *Effects of the Change from Rate-of-Return to Price-Cap Regulation*, 83 AM. ECON. REV. PAPERS & PROC. 191 (1993); Ronald R. Braeutigam & John C. Panzar, *Diversification Incentives Under "Price-Based" and "Cost-Based" Regulation*, 20 RAND J. ECON. 373, 387-90 (1989).

grasp of the firm's true costs, but they do know the historic pattern of telephone prices. Any large upward deviation from trends brought about by large-scale LEC subsidization of video would surely attract regulatory attention and public protest.

Much the same can be said for traditional rate-of-return regulation. The firm cannot immediately pass on any and all costs to its monopoly ratepayers. Typically, the firm is allowed only a portion of the cost pass-through that it seeks, and then only after long and tortuous review in a formal rate case. Indeed, the hope of reducing the administrative costs and time delays associated with rate-of-return regulation has driven regulatory agencies to adopt a price-cap or other incentive regulation scheme.

Competitive Access to the Network. Other regulatory tools are designed specifically to reduce monopoly power—the potential source of subsidies by the LECs—by requiring access to portions of the network by competitive providers. A leading example is the introduction of open network architecture (ONA) by the LECs. LECs are being required to unbundle the various parts of their networks and make them available to outsiders under reasonable terms. Accordingly, users are able to assemble their own networks by selecting components from an LEC under ONA access requirements.

Devising the ONA requirements has been a long and difficult process, with many criticisms that they do not break through the LECs' monopoly bottlenecks.[66] Modification of ONA requirements based on experience and formal complaints, however, may strengthen the effectiveness of this regulatory tool. A learning process for both regulators and the industry is involved. Over time, ONA requirements may progressively improve, with the LEC's ability to cross-subsidize correspondingly reduced.

Especially important, the FCC has adopted rules to facilitate expanded interconnection by LECs with local competitive access providers (CAPs) and other entities for both special access and

---

66. Relevant FCC decisions and filings by interested parties are in CC Dkt. No. 89-79. For detailed criticism of the effectiveness of ONA requirements, see HATFIELD ASSOCIATES, NEW LOCAL EXCHANGE TECHNOLOGY: PRESERVING THE BOTTLENECK OR PROVIDING COMPETITIVE ALTERNATIVES? (Apr. 6, 1992); HUBER, KELLOGG & THORNE, *supra* note 63, at 2.46-.48.

switched services.[67] A growing number of states are also mandating requirements for interconnection between LECs and competitive access providers for intrastate services.[68] Enforcement of interconnection requirements will strengthen competitors by affording direct access to LEC switches and trunking facilities.

Market Pressures. Combined with regulatory tools, evolving market pressures are reducing the ability of LECs to cross-subsidize. The threat of cross-subsidization is constrained because the pool of potential LEC monopoly revenues available to absorb cost shifting is shrinking. Some services that were monopolies in past decades are becoming increasingly competitive. As just two examples, CAPs are using fiber networks to compete with LECs for local business traffic,[69] while customer-supplied private branch exchange (PBX) equipment is a competitive alternative to LEC centrex service. As cable operators themselves enter narrowband markets, they will contribute to the erosion of the LECs' monopoly, reducing further the dangers of LEC cross-subsidization.

Many have speculated that the development of personal communications networks (PCNs) will eventually provide a competitive alternative to the local loop. If so, the LECs' core monopoly would disappear. It would be unwise to place great reliance in policy making on the expectation that PCNs, now in early development, will eventually become such widespread competitors to the LECs that the local exchange bottleneck will vanish. But it remains important to recognize the emergence of substitutes for use of the LECs' network, including the possibilities afforded by PCN technologies.

That opportunities for cross-subsidization may be overshadowed by other considerations in corporate decision making is suggested by the move of Pacific Telesis to spin off into an entirely separate publicly

---

67. *See* Expanded Interconnection with Local Telephone Company Facilities, Report and Order, and Notice of Proposed Rulemaking, CC Dkt. Nos. 91-141, 92-222, 7 F.C.C. Rcd. 7369 (1992) (adopting rules for expanded interconnection for special access services); Expanded Interconnection with Local Telephone Company Facilities, Second Report and Order, and Third Notice of Proposed Rulemaking, CC Dkt. Nos. 91-141, 80-286, 8 F.C.C. Rcd. 7374 (1993) (adopting rules of expanded interconnection for switched access).

68. For a survey of state experiences, see ILLINOIS COMMERCE COMMISSION, LOCAL COMPETITION AND INTERCONNECTION (July 1, 1992).

69. For a state-by-state compilation of CAP activities, see HUBER, KELLOGG & THORNE, *supra* note 63, at 2.37-.38.

traded corporation its regulated companies, Pacific Bell and Nevada Bell, from its other holding company subsidiaries, which include its domestic and foreign cellular operations.[70] If cross-subsidization were of dominant importance, this action by Pacific Telesis would be contrary to what one would expect. The concept of cross-subsidization rests on the notion of a single entity being able to shift costs between activities—a shift that is impossible when these activities are separated by divestiture.

Recapitulation. Three points are key. First, the ability of LECs to cross-subsidize is being weakened by regulatory tools and evolving competitive pressures. Among regulatory tools, accounting rules are useful primarily because common-cost allocations provide a safety margin against underestimates of incremental cost. Price caps and other forms of incentive regulation weaken (but do not eliminate) the ability of the LEC to raise telephone rates in response to financial losses in other markets.

Second, the erosion of telephone monopoly markets is centrally important in reducing the threat of cross-subsidy. With expanded interconnection requirements and other developments, competitive pressures in the LECs' core markets will continue to increase. The threat of cross-subsidy is less today than previously, and it will continue to diminish.

Third, at any given time, the threat of cross-subsidization will vary among markets, depending on how LECs view their opportunities within a large portfolio of alternative strategic actions. Some LECs may be so squeezed financially that they would not seriously contemplate subsidization of video, even if the prospects for long-term payoff were bright. Others may have greater financial leeway but decide that video is not a good candidate for subsidization in light of opportunities elsewhere. Yet others may conclude that entry into video is so vital to remaining at the cutting edge of telecommunications technologies that they must pursue ventures, even at great risk to their telephone ratepayers. Each situation must be judged by the conditions at hand. The Commission's decisions will rest on tough judgment calls.

70. PACIFIC TELESIS GROUP, 1992 SEC FORM 10-K, at 4-10 (1993).

The InterLATA Restriction

Under the line-of-business restrictions specified in the MFJ, the RBOCs and BOCs are barred from providing interLATA telecommunications services or manufacturing telecommunications equipment.[71] Without a waiver, the BOC is not permitted to transport video programming across LATA boundaries within its operating territory, nor is an RBOC permitted to do so outside its operating territory (if, for example, it acquires an out-of-territory cable system). Among the problems posed by the ban, the BOC is not permitted to place in one LATA a video server interconnected with video networks in other LATAs. If a large server has a lower per-user cost than a small one, the inability of the BOC to take advantage of scale economies would handicap the BOC in competing with cable operators who are not so constrained.

In practice, the BOCs and RBOCs may succeed in obtaining the necessary court waivers on a case-by-case basis for such interLATA activities—but at the expense of considerable time delays and uncertainty. In September 1993, for example, U.S. District Court Judge Harold Greene granted Southwestern Bell a waiver for use with the cable franchises that it purchased from Hauser Communications in the Washington, D.C. area,[72] seven months after the planned purchase was announced. In February 1993, Bell Atlantic filed a request for a waiver to transport video programming within its operating territory without regard to LATA boundaries.[73] A year later, the court's decision had not been handed down.

Critical here are the conditions specified in the MFJ under which line-of-business restrictions are to be lifted.[74] Section VIII(C) of the Decree specifies that restrictions are to be removed on a showing "that

71. Modification of Final Judgment, United States *v.* American Tel. & Tel. Co., 552 F. Supp. 131, 225-34 (D.D.C. 1982); *see also* KELLOGG, THORNE & HUBER, *supra* note 21, at 291-342. The MFJ originally included a ban also on BOC provision of information services. That restriction was lifted in 1991. United States v. Western Elec. Co., No. 82-0192 (D.D.C. July 25, 1991), *aff'd,* 993 F.2d 1572 (D.C. Cir. 1993).

72. TELECOMMUNICATIONS REP., Sept. 27, 1993, at 31.

73. Defendant's Motion for Waiver, United States *v.* Western Elec. Co., No. 82-0192 (filed Feb. 26, 1993) (requesting waiver to provide video programming service without regard to LATA boundaries).

74. For an extended discussion, see KELLOGG, THORNE & HUBER, *supra* note 21, at 362-72.

there is no substantial possibility" that the BOC "could use its monopoly power to impede competition in the market it seeks to enter." The Court of Appeals later ruled that "unless the entering BOC will have the ability to raise prices or restrict output in the market it seeks to enter, there can be no substantial possibility that it could use its monopoly power to 'impede competition.'"[75]

To assess the relevance of this language for video transport, let us consider separately the in-territory and out-of-territory situations faced by the BOCs and the RBOCs. With respect to construction of an integrated network by a BOC to compete with an incumbent cable operator, the BOC certainly has "no monopoly power in the [video] market it seeks to enter." As Chapter 3 emphasizes, the LECs will face an uphill struggle to compete with cable incumbents. Whatever market power is wielded today is in the hands of the cable incumbents. Indeed, their market power provided the basis for reregulation of the cable industry under the 1992 Cable Act. The market power of the LECs in local telephony (especially to residential and small business users) bears no similarity to the situation faced by the LECs in the local video market in competition not only with cable operators but also with DBS and wireless multichannel systems, broadcasting stations, and video cassette stores.

Perhaps some would argue that, with the LECs' ability to cross-subsidize, they could drive out the cable rival and, thus, "impede competition." However, if the LECs have such strong ability to cross-subsidize that they would quickly dominate the local video market, the appropriate remedy is to reverse FCC's decision that permits LECs to offer video dialtone or, more precisely, to prohibit the LECs from offering video except through networks wholly separate from their telephone networks. For, as we have seen, it is the joint use of the network by video and telephone services that breeds the problem of cross-subsidy. LEC entry into video dialtone (with presumed use of integrated transmission facilities) is based on the FCC's belief that safeguards against cross-subsidization are adequate or can be made so on the basis of continuing review. If, however, the threat of cross-subsidy is perceived by the courts and by Congress to be so serious that the general ban on interLATA transport of video signals should not be lifted, the fundamental underpinning for the FCC's video dialtone

75. United States *v.* Western Elec. Co., 900 F.2d 283, 296 (D.C. Cir.), *cert. denied,* 498 U.S. 911 (1990).

decision itself would be called into question.

With respect to out-of-territory operations, suppose that an RBOC acquires a distant cable system. Does the RBOC have the ability to impede competition in that market to a greater degree than would the incumbent cable operator had it remained unattached to the RBOC? In other words, is there something special about the RBOCs (a characteristic not shared with cable operators or non-Bell telephone companies) that would pose a competitive threat in out-of-territory video markets? If the answer is yes, the RBOC should not be permitted to acquire the cable system in the first place. The issue of interLATA transport of video programming is of trivial importance in this determination.

The root difficulty stems from the fact that the crafters of the MFJ were concerned with the *telephone* market, not the video market. It was the local telephone market, not the video market, where the LECs were alleged to have monopoly power. It was the telephone market, not the video market, where the BOCs were alleged to have bottleneck facilities that could be used to favor their affiliated interexchange carrier (AT&T Long Lines) at the expense of other interexchange carriers. When a LATA was defined in section IV(G) of the Decree as "one or more contiguous local exchange areas servicing common social, economic, and other purposes," the reference was to telephone exchanges, not to cable headends. For the BOCs and RBOCs, the video market is wildly different from the telephone market. To permit them entry into video, through video dialtone or out-of-territory cable ventures, but then to handicap them with an irrelevant interLATA restriction, is a stark demonstration of how historical accidents can adversely affect public policy.

Conclusions

The LECs will face great difficulty in competing with incumbent cable operators, at least during this decade, even if they have the same freedom of action as cable operators do in the video marketplace. They will face even greater difficulty if they are burdened with video dialtone obligations while cable operators retain their freedom to operate as non–common carriers.

Moreover, if the LECs, as a consequence of technological advances, are able to compete effectively even if limited to video dialtone, the use of the LEC video platform may evolve in ways that will defeat the Commission's objective of video common carriage. For this reason, the long-term viability of video dialtone is questionable.

If video common carriage is not achieved, however, society may suffer no serious consequences. Information diversity would not necessarily grow under the rules of common carriage. Moreover, the increasing number of video channels being made available to the American public will expand programming choices with or without common carriage. Finally, competition from nonwireline carriers, considered in later chapters, will further encourage program diversity, even though none operates as a common carrier.

The LECs have leeway to cross-subsidize by understating their incremental costs in ways that regulators will be hard pressed to detect. The key safeguards against cross-subsidization are allocations of common cost to video that provide a safety margin against under-estimates of video incremental cost, erosion of the LECs' traditional monopoly markets through competitive entry, and price cap and other forms of incentive regulation. These safeguards, however, do not eliminate but only mitigate the problem. We must expect the threat of cross-subsidy to vary among the LECs depending on their particular financial situations and the range of their perceived business opportunities, video being only one.

Finally, the ban on interLATA transmission of video by the Bell operating companies arose for reasons having nothing to do with the video market. Regardless of public policy decisions about the interLATA ban on information transmission more generally, the video portion should be scraped as one step (albeit a small one) toward reforming the ground rules for competition between the LECs and cable operators.

5

Lifting the Cross-Ownership Ban
for Local Telephone Companies

HAVING EXPLORED THE PROSPECTS for video dialtone as constrained by the cross-ownership ban, we turn to the potential consequences of lifting the ban. Without the ban, the LECs (through their
parent telephone companies) would be free to own programming—that
is, to integrate vertically into the supply of programming. Moreover,
depending on the nature of continuing restrictions, they could move
away from nondiscriminatory common carriage and enjoy the same
freedom that cable operators have in dealing with program suppliers.
At this writing, legislative initiatives by Congress are being directed to
lifting the ban, while challenges to the ban's constitutionality are proceeding in the courts.

In response to these legislative and courtroom activities, we consider
the consequences of lifting the ban. Of central concern is the relationship between LEC ownership of programming and the threats of cross-
subsidization and anticompetitive use of network bottlenecks. We then
assess three potential safeguards: (1) regulatory limits on horizontal
concentration, (2) limits on channel occupancy by affiliated programmers, and (3) obligations to maintain nondiscriminatory access to channels. Finally, we examine three other topics relevant to removal of the
cross-ownership ban: (1) prohibitions against buyouts of cable systems
by LECs in their service territories, (2) the effects of LEC involvement
on information diversity, and (3) regulatory parity for competition in
telephony.

Cross-Subsidization, Network Bottlenecks, and Program Ownership

Concerns about cross-subsidization have been persistently voiced in debates about lifting the ban and the nature of needed safeguards without it. In describing legislation to lift the ban, for example, Congressman Rick Boucher emphasizes that "in order to ensure that there is no cross-subsidization, we require a common carrier that wants to provide video programming directly to subscribers in its telephone service area to establish a video programming affiliate that is separate from the carrier, and that will maintain separate books, records, and accounts."[1]

At the outset, it is important to recognize that the mechanics of cross-subsidization for LEC integration into programming are quite different from the mechanics depicted in Chapter 4 for video dialtone. The root of the cross-subsidy problem lies in the joint use of the network by telephone and video services (recall the electronics package example in Chapter 4). In contrast, outlays for program production and distribution are easily distinguishable from those for transmission of video and telephone signals. Thus, the separation of accounts and records is straightforward, and the challenge of estimating incremental costs does not intrude. In this sense, the involvement of a telephone company in video programming would be no different from the multitude of its other activities—be they in real estate, financial services, or retailing of telecommunications equipment.

What does set programming apart from these other activities is that programming would be an input into the video services (programming plus transmission) provided by LECs to subscribers. The key issue is whether this phenomenon of self-dealing would lead to undesirable outcomes. Two possibilities merit exploration: Self-dealing (1) facilitates evasion of the regulatory limitation on the LEC's profits and (2) encourages anticompetitive use of the LEC's network bottleneck.

Evasion of the Profit Constraint. If the regulated firm diversifies into an unregulated market that supplies inputs to the firm's regulated activities, the firm has an opportunity to evade the regulatory limitation

---

1. 139 Cong. Rec. E799, E799 (daily ed. Mar. 30, 1993) (statement of Rep. Boucher).

on its profits. It pays excessive amounts for the input (thereby increasing its profits in the nonregulated market) and, with rate-of-return regulation, compensates by increasing its prices in the regulated market. With successful cost shifting, the firm is left with higher profits in the unregulated market, no diminution of profits in its regulated activities, and higher prices paid by subscribers for its regulated services. Thus, subscribers would pay, in effect, a subsidy in the form of higher prices but with the payments contributing simply to the firm's profits.

Recall, in a similar vein, how concerns about the tie between AT&T and Western Electric (which led to the consent decree of 1956 and to the MFJ in 1982) arose in part from allegations that AT&T was paying excessive prices for telephone equipment from Western Electric as a way to increase profits.[2] But note a critical difference. The vertical tie of concern here is between the LEC's video portion of its transmission system (not its telephone portion) and its affiliated programming. Any subsidies from captive telephone ratepayers would have to flow from the telephone to the video portion of the transmission system, *then* to the affiliated programming.

To illustrate, consider a LEC that succeeds in extracting an additional $100 from its telephone subscribers by understating the incremental cost of video transmission, as discussed in Chapter 4. It succeeds in fooling regulators into permitting a $100 increase in telephone revenues to cover the $100 in cost shifted from the video portion to the telephone portion of the integrated network. To simplify the analysis, let us suppose (not unrealistically) that the video transmission portion operates as a separate subsidiary of the LEC. The video transmission subsidiary now has an additional $100, which can be regarded as a subsidy from telephone subscribers.

What does the video subsidiary do with the $100? One possibility is that it simply keeps it as an additional profit for the benefit of itself and its parent telephone company. But something is amiss here. The

---

2. United States *v.* Western Elec. Co., 1956 Trade Cas. (CCH) ¶ 68,246 (D.N.J. 1956). For a treatment of the concerns voiced about the AT&T-Western Electric tie between the time of the 1956 and 1982 judicial actions, see PRESIDENT'S TASK FORCE ON COMMUNICATIONS POLICY (G.P.O. 1968); MICHAEL J. KELLOGG, JOHN THORNE & PETER W. HUBER, FEDERAL TELECOMMUNICATIONS LAW 202-10 (Little, Brown & Co. 1992).

LEC has succeeded in evading the profit constraint without any connection to ownership interests in programming or to the cross-ownership ban. This illustration is wholly consistent with the operation of video dialtone, with the cross-ownership ban in place, described in Chapter 4. The cross-ownership ban turns out to be irrelevant to questions about evasion of the regulatory profit constraint. If safeguards against cross-subsidization are weak, the LEC can enhance its profits without ownership of programming. If the safeguards are strong, the LEC has no way to extract a subsidy from telephone users, with or without ownership in programming.

Instead of retaining the $100 as additional profit to the benefit of shareholders, the LEC could, for example, increase its managers' salaries or invest in overseas ventures, or reduce rates to video subscribers as a way to undercut the incumbent cable operator as a predatory strategy described in Chapter 4. In all cases, the subsidy arises from the confounding of costs incurred in transmitting video and telephone signals on the same network, not from anything to do with ownership of programming.

What effect, then, does ownership of programming have on outcomes? Program ownership would give the video transmission subsidiary more choices in deciding how to spend the $100. One possibility is especially notable. Suppose the video subsidiary, seeking more subscribers, spends the money to improve the quality of programming and to support the production of programming that otherwise would not exist. This action would directly contribute to program diversity, valued at the Commission and elsewhere. This enhancement, however, would be at the expense of telephone subscribers. Is this outcome, on balance, good or bad? So far we have considered cross-subsidy in a negative, anticompetitive sense. But subsidies would not necessarily be devoted to ill purpose. The example here would involve the same substantive outcome as a tax on telephone service levied by a municipality, with the proceeds used by the municipality to support the performing arts (or perhaps public libraries) to a greater degree than otherwise. We leave it to the reader to judge the merits of such outcomes and return to the subject of program diversity and LEC involvement later in this chapter.

Anticompetitive Use of the Network

Continuing the illustration, we might imagine the video transmission subsidiary using the $100 to help fund a strategy to discriminate in favor of its program affiliates. It would do so by charging its affiliates lower network access fees than those to outsiders, with the $100 subsidy used to offset the revenue loss from the lowered access fee. Alternatively, the affiliated-programmer access fee could be kept constant, the access fees to outsiders raised, and the $100 subsidy used to offset the loss of business from these outsiders. The LEC's objective would be to handicap outside program suppliers that depend on the LECs bottleneck network as a means to help its parent telephone company dominate the nationwide program supply market.[3] Three scenarios illustrate such a chain of events: (1) a LEC is free to buy out incumbent cable systems in its telephone service area but not elsewhere; (2) all buyouts are prohibited; and (3) such buyouts are prohibited in a LEC's telephone service area but permitted elsewhere.

A LEC Local Buyout. As an extreme case, suppose that all LECs were simply to buy out the incumbent cable systems within their telephone service territories, with full freedom to operate the cable systems as they are operated today. Thus, households continue to be served by only one video wireline (abstracting from the few cases of overbuilds discussed in Chapter 2). Assume further that the number of homes passed by cable in each territory as a percentage of homes passed nationwide is equal to the number of residential telephone access lines in that territory as a percentage of total residential access lines nationwide. In this case, each RBOC and GTE would have video access ranging from about 9 to 14 percent of the nation's households passed by cable; numerous small independent telephone companies would collectively account for another 7 percent.[4]

Consider an RBOC, say, carrier *C*, which, under the above assumptions, has video wireline access to 12 percent of the nation's

---

3. *See, e.g.,* Affidavit of Bruce M. Owen (May 20, 1993), Chesapeake & Potomac Tel. Co. *v.* United States, 830 F. Supp. 909 (E.D. Va. 1993).

4. These estimates are based on the number of residential access lines reported in FEDERAL COMMUNICATIONS COMMISSION, STATISTICS OF COMMUNICATIONS COMMON CARRIERS, 1991-1992, at 157-68 (1992).

homes. The programming market is competitive with numerous suppliers offering material of national interest. Carrier *C* vertically integrates with program suppliers, group *D*. Carrier *C* proceeds to discriminate in favor of group *D* by charging *D* less for access to its local networks than it charges other program suppliers. Carrier *C* might also provide outside suppliers with inferior transmission (they complain, but only weeks later are "technical" difficulties fixed), place outsiders less favorably in the channel lineup, delay service to some who request it, and, in other ways, put these suppliers at a disadvantage. Because of discriminatory treatment in the 12 percent of the national video wireline market controlled by carrier *C*, many outside suppliers become so weakened that they merge with group *D* or go out of business. With its increasing market power in national programming, carrier *C* extracts, through its group *D* affiliate, more favorable terms from other RBOCs and independent telephone companies that have become highly dependent on group *D* for programming.

No more than a moment's reflection is needed to appreciate the implausibility of this scenario. It would be hard for *C* to weaken nonaffiliated suppliers by discriminatory treatment, because other carriers (covering 88 percent of the homes passed by cable) would be playing the same game by proceeding to discriminate against *D* in favor of their own affiliates. Competition among carriers seeking to gain market power in the program supply market would make it difficult for any to succeed.

To make the bottleneck–program-domination scenario plausible, carrier *C* must cover a large portion of the nation's households, and other carriers must fail to prevent it from proceeding with its plans. The scenario would be more plausible if, by merging with other telephone companies, carrier *C* obtained, say, a 30 percent share of homes passed, while other carriers had only fragmented shares that frustrated their coordinated action against *C*.

Three points emerge from this scenario. First, of critical importance is a limitation on horizontal concentration permitted to any one carrier. If a 30 percent share is enough to trigger legitimate concerns of anticompetitive behavior, an obvious remedy would involve a limitation by the FCC or Congress on the number of households to which a single telephone company could have video access. Indeed, the Commission, at the behest of Congress, has already established horizontal concentration limits on the cable industry,[5] discussed below.

Second, the tie between cross-subsidization and the threat of market dominance in programming is tenuous. As earlier illustrated, channeling the $100 subsidy from telephone subscribers to finance the LECs discriminatory practices toward programming affiliates is only one of many ways the subsidy might be used.

If the threat of anticompetitive use of bottlenecks is serious, the appropriate remedy is to impose limits on horizontal concentration, not to single out the LECs for prohibitions against program ownership. If potential cross-subsidies are deemed so large that they greatly enhance the ability of LECs (unlike today's cable operators) to behave anticompetitively in program markets, the appropriate remedy is to tackle the cross-subsidy problem directly. This task would involve either strengthening the safeguards against cross-subsidization or, if that would be hopeless, reversing the FCC's decision to permit the LECs to offer video dialtone even with the cross-ownership ban in place. If the safeguards are strong enough (or can be made so), as the FCC concluded in its video dialtone decision, then no additional concern would be warranted on cross-subsidy grounds for the LECs' further move into programming. Whatever threat of anticompetitive behavior exists in programming markets would apply no less to today's cable operators that have no captive telephone market.

A counterargument is that integration into programming does exacerbate the problem of cross-subsidy by making LEC entry into video more profitable.[6] If the LEC is constrained only to video dialtone in line with this reasoning, it may choose not to enter the video market because of the poor prospects for success. In this case, no cross-subsidy would emerge simply because entry does not take place. Only with integration into programming would the LEC proceed, and only in that case would the specter of cross-subsidy arise. This is an odd argument.

---

5. Implementation of Sections 11 and 13 of the Cable Television Consumer Protection and Competition Act of 1992, Horizontal and Vertical Ownership Limits, Second Report and Order, MM Dkt. No. 92-264, 8 F.C.C. Rcd. 8565 (1993) [hereinafter *Horizontal and Vertical Ownership Limits*].

6. *See, e.g.,* Affidavit of Bruce M. Owen (June 9, 1993), Chesapeake & Potomac Tel. Co. *v.* United States, 830 F. Supp. 909 (E.D. Va. 1993).

It's like saying that the LEC should be allowed to compete in providing cable service—but only between the hours of 12 A.M. and 12 P.M. To permit round-the-clock service would raise the probability that the LEC would enter the video market and, thus, would raise the probability of cross-subsidy.

Third, measurements of market share must take into account the nature of the relevant market. The above illustrations are based on the assumption that the relevant program market is national in scope. This assumption is consistent with filings before the Commission arguing that "most programming distribution occurs on a national, not a regional, basis" and that "there is no evidence that cable operators possess market power in the local advertising or program acquisition markets . . . [because] the power of cable operators in these markets continues to lag behind local broadcasting stations."[7] As one example, the National Cable Television Association emphasizes that "the market in which cable operators buy, and cable programmers sell, is essentially national in scope. Absent any clear indication to the contrary, the imposition of regional subscriber limits is neither required nor appropriate."[8]

In cases where markets are regional or local in nature or become increasingly so as the video arena evolves, limitations on horizontal concentration should be tied to the appropriate smaller geographical areas for such programming. In this connection, a characteristic—aside from cross-subsidy concerns—that does set the LECs apart from cable operators is the geographical concentration of LEC transmission facilities. The BOCs are far more concentrated within their operating territories than even the largest cable MSOs in the same territories. Within New York City, for example, New York Telephone has a share of local exchange service (essentially 100 percent) far greater than the share of cable service held in New York City by any single MSO. Under terms of our scenario, a buyout by a BOC of all cable systems in its territory would result in a greatly increased market share for video service held by a single entity within that local geographical area. For local programming, where broadcasting stations would be the

7. *Horizontal and Vertical Ownership Limits, supra* note 5, at ¶ 15.
8. National Cable Television Ass'n, Comments, MM Dkt. No. 92-264, at 19 (Feb. 9, 1993).

rivals primarily disadvantaged by the LEC's anticompetitive behavior, a limitation on LEC affiliations with local program suppliers might be appropriate. But, again, the basis of the limitation would rest not on the threat of cross-subsidization but on the LEC's control of access required by local programmers. The same remedy would be appropriate for cable operators who have, or might obtain, large market shares for video wireline access within specific metropolitan areas.

All Buyouts Prohibited. In contrast to our first scenario, here the LECs are foreclosed by law from entering the video business by acquiring existing cable systems. They may enter only by building their own video transmission facilities, presumably in conjunction with their telephone service. Thus, they face the full presence of incumbent cable rivals.

Using the local bottleneck for leverage into programming dominance is even less plausible here than in the first scenario, because in this case there is no bottleneck. With programmers having access to the incumbent cable operators, the LEC would have no monopoly of local transmission to exploit. The most we can imagine is the LEC eventually becoming such a powerful competitor, perhaps through cross-subsidization and predation, that it drives out cable incumbents. With such success, it would achieve a monopoly of local wireline access that could then be exploited in the programming arena. But this simply brings us back to the first scenario. There the LECs also have a wireline monopoly. But their ability to exploit it is seriously constrained so long as the parent company of each has only a small national market share of wireline access.

Local Buyouts Prohibited, Out-of-Territory Cable Acquisitions Permitted. Suppose each RBOC or independent telephone company seeks to provide video service in its own territory through its LECs, while simultaneously entering into partnerships with or acquiring one or more cable MSOs. An obvious model was the planned merger of Bell Atlantic, TCI, and Liberty Media. TCI (including Liberty) passes about 27 percent of the nation's homes.[9] Let us assume that TCI and Liberty cable properties in Bell Atlantic's territory would have been sold if the merger had been consummated. Assume further that Bell Atlantic

9. *Horizontal and Vertical Ownership Limits, supra* note 5, at 8578 n.40.

would have purchased out-of-territory cable systems to offset the loss of in-territory cable coverage, so that the merged entity would have continued to pass 27 percent of the nation's homes.[10] Moreover, Bell Atlantic's LECs could enter the video market within its territory encompassing 13 percent of the nation's actual and potential cable subscribers.[11] Thus, the combination would have had access to 40 percent of the nation's homes.

Bell Atlantic, however, would have faced well-entrenched cable incumbents in its territory. As in the second scenario, its LECs would have no monopoly network bottleneck that could be used for leverage in the national programming market. If Bell Atlantic were somehow able to achieve a dominant position in its territory by driving out or greatly weakening the incumbents, its level of concentration would be much more worrisome. We could imagine Bell Atlantic achieving essentially monopoly wireline control to some 40 percent of the nation's households, with attendant greater prospects of leveraging its power into programming if the cross-ownership ban were lifted.

But this outcome is far-fetched. Other RBOCs and independent telephone companies would likely seek partnerships with MSOs, as well as with video programmers, software firms, and others. If Bell Atlantic's LECs were so successful in competing with and driving out incumbent cable operators, we must expect the LECs of other RBOCs also to achieve success in gaining video dominance in their own territories against incumbent cable operators, including those owned by Bell Atlantic or other out-of-territory RBOCs. In other words, we would expect that Bell Atlantic's gains in the in-territory video market share achieved by its LECs would be at least partially offset by its out-of-territory losses to no-less-powerful LECs. Thus, the scenario of the single RBOC gaining a nationwide wireline monopoly market share of up to 40 percent, by virtue of merging with the nation's longest MSO, lacks plausibility.

10. TCI and Liberty have affiliations in Bell Atlantic's territory with 110 cable systems with nearly 2 million subscribers, comprising 15 percent of their nationwide subscriber base. TELECOMMUNICATIONS REP., Oct. 18, 1993, at 3.

11. The 13 percent figure is taken from the number of homes passed by cable in Bell Atlantic's territory (10.5 million) divided by the number of homes passed by cable nationally (78.7 million). NATIONAL CABLE TELEVISION ASS'N, CABLE TELEVISION DEVELOPMENTS 13-A (Mar. 1993).

The lesson from this third scenario is that the merger of an RBOC and a major MSO is not by itself anticompetitive. Indeed, in two ways such mergers are *procompetitive*. First, the out-of-territory RBOC (or independent telephone company) strengthens the ability of its partnering incumbent cable systems to move into telephony in competition with the in-territory LECs of another parent telephone company. Second, the LECs of that parent telephone company would be better able to move into video in competition with incumbent cable operators. In short, participants on both sides of the market become stronger rivals.

Of critical importance, again, is the degree of horizontal concentration. In the first scenario, a straight buyout of cable systems by telephone companies in their own territories would not lead to frightening outcomes in potential programming domination because no one telephone entity would have more than about 13 percent of the cable market. In contrast, when out-of-territory purchases are considered in the third scenario, the cable market share can go far higher. In the unsuccessful Bell Atlantic–TCI merger, Bell Atlantic would have held perhaps 27 percent of the cable market (in terms of TCI's then-current share of homes passed, with possible restructuring, as discussed earlier). Other strategic alliances could push further the degree of horizontal concentration. A number of MSOs merged with an RBOC, or two RBOCs joining forces, could lead to far more troubling outcomes.

Limitations on Horizontal Concentration

Congress, long concerned about horizontal concentration in the cable industry, directed the Commission in the 1992 Cable Act to set limits on the number of cable subscribers served by a single entity.[12] In response, the Commission has established a 30 percent limit on "the number of homes passed nationwide that any one entity can reach through cable systems in which such entity has an attributable interest."[13] The decision has been stayed, pending the outcome of appeals

---

12. 47 U.S.C. § 533(f)(1)(A).

13. *Horizontal and Vertical Ownership Limits*, *supra* note 5, at 8567 ¶ 3. The limitation is set at 35 percent if the entity is minority-owned. The Commission adopted a homes-passed standard rather than a subscriber standard on grounds that a measure based

to a district court decision that this provision of the 1992 Cable Act, requiring the Commission to set subscriber limits, is unconstitutional.[14]

Setting to one side the court action, we must ask whether the 30 percent limitation established by the Commission is too high. The basis for that choice was, in part, arguments by interested parties that "many cable programming services have flourished at subscriber penetration levels well below 60 percent."[15] By implication, even if 30 percent of the market had been foreclosed because of discriminatory treatment by a cable operator with a 30 percent market share, these programming services would have succeeded. But this line of reasoning is troubling for three reasons. First, by focusing only on the successes, it does not count the services that failed as a consequence of limited access to cable systems. It is easy to imagine services that fail to get off the ground, even if they would have conferred net benefits to the viewing public, because of inadequate access to cable systems.

Second, the issue is not just of success or failure but of the quality of programming. Although a service might break even at, say, 60 percent penetration, a higher level of penetration may encourage better or more varied programming.

Third, and most important, the multiplication of channels in the coming years will result in progressively greater audience fragmentation. Individual program services, competing with many dozens or hundreds of others, will need access to a progressively larger number of cable systems if a sufficient audience is to be accumulated to cover costs. Even if access to cable systems encompassing 60 percent of the nation's cable subscribers suffices today for many programmers, an 80 percent or 90 percent figure may be required as we move into a world of hundreds of channels.

In the other direction, emerging competition in local video markets, weakening the bottleneck held by the local cable operator (possibly an out-of-territory RBOC), will reduce the importance of horizontal concentration by MSOs. Even if an MSO had, say, a 40 percent nation-

---

on the number of subscribers is relatively unstable and may also serve to discourage subscriber growth. *Id.* at 8574 ¶ 19.

14. Daniels Cablevision, Inc. *v.* United States, 835 F. Supp. 1 (D.D.C. 1993).

15. *Horizontal and Vertical Ownership Limits*, *supra* note 5, at 8575 ¶ 22.

wide market share, the situation would be tolerable if these systems faced vigorous competition from wireless systems, discussed in later chapters, and from in-territory LECs.

Moreover, what about possible losses in scale economies with limitations on horizontal concentration? Is an MSO with a large market share likely to operate more efficiently than one with a small share? Although it is reasonable to suppose that limitations to very small shares would reduce economic efficiency, nothing in the Commission's record suggests that a limitation to, say, 20 percent would cause economic harm that would be avoided with the higher 30 percent limitation.

With these currents and countercurrents, and with the critical role played by horizontal concentration, the Commission should revisit its decision to select a 30 percent limitation. Among its tasks, it should ask whether a lower limit of perhaps 20 percent would be preferable on grounds of promising an additional safety margin against anticompetitive behavior. In doing so, it should inquire into how the greater presence of the RBOCs in out-of-territory video markets would affect the answer.

Finally, antitrust enforcement has a critical role alongside well-conceived structural safeguards. The preceding scenarios were all based on the assumptions that the major players behave independently of each other. But collusion among large telephone companies and cable MSOs could radically alter the outcomes in terms of anticompetitive threats. Vigilance against collusive behavior is all the more important in light of the numerous alliances being announced among groups of players.[16] Questions will persist about whether alliances among either cable companies or telephone companies, say, to develop new software or to establish technical compatibility standards, encourage anticompetitive behavior.

At the same time, it would seem unwise to rely entirely on antitrust safeguards as a substitute for structural restrictions. Antitrust enforcement involves time-consuming and costly fact-finding processes frequently triggered only after a serious violation is alleged. Difficult

---

16. Consider, for example, the agreement among the five largest cable MSOs to form a joint venture to offer PCS and other telephone services. *See* TELECOMMUNICATIONS REP., Dec. 6, 1993, at 3-4.

decisions are required about appropriate remedies involving, for example, divestiture and grandfathering of existing market relationships. By helping to forestall antitrust violations, well-conceived structural safeguards may provide the stitch in time that, indeed, saves nine.

Channel-Occupancy Limits

The 1992 Cable Act also requires, as another safeguard, the Commission to establish reasonable limits on the number of cable channels that may be occupied by programmers affiliated with cable operators.[17] In response, the Commission has decided that a cable operator may fill no more than 40 percent of the system's active capacity with affiliated programming. This limit applies in cases of up to seventy-five channels. Beyond that cap, channel use remains unfettered.

Occupancy limits are potentially less effective than limitations on horizontal concentration. A cable operator could conceivably have ownership interests in many channels carried over the system. Yet, if the operator has only a small national market share of local cable access, no leverage would exist for anticompetitive behavior in programming. But the reverse is not necessarily true. Suppose that (1) the cable operator carries only a few channels of affiliated programming and (2) this programming comprises a large portion of a type of programming that has no close substitutes (for example, a set of popular pay movie channels, home shopping channels, or national and international news channels). With a large share of cable local access, the cable operator could discriminate against nonaffiliated programmers for that type of programming.[18] It could thereby strengthen the position of its own affiliates in the national market, enabling it to extract additional profits from other cable operators.

Channel-occupancy limits are a potentially useful backstop if limits on horizontal concentration are set too high. In any event, whatever channel-occupancy limits are established for cable operators could be carried over to the LECs, as one more safeguard with removal of the cross-ownership ban.

17. 47 U.S.C. § 533(f)(1)(B).
18. *Horizontal and Vertical Ownership Limits, supra* note 5, at 8567 ¶ 4.

Nondiscriminatory Channel Access

Despite the above safeguards, which are already in place for cable operators and could be made applicable also to the LECs if the cross-ownership ban were lifted, strong pressures remain for singling out the LECs for further protection against anticompetitive behavior. Congressional legislation introduced in 1993, while lifting the cross-ownership ban, would impose on the LECs' programming limitations to which cable operators are not subject. S. 1086 stipulates that any video programming provided by the LEC be offered to subscribers only through a separate subsidiary and under a tariff approved by the FCC.[19] H.R. 1504 stipulates that the LEC may provide programming only "through a separate programming affiliate that is separate from such carrier."[20] Moreover, any LEC that provides,

> through a video programming affiliate, video programming directly to subscribers in its telephone service area shall establish a video platform. The Commission, together with the States, shall establish regulations to prohibit a carrier from discriminating in favor of its video programming affiliate in providing access to such platform or with regard to rates, terms, and conditions for access to such platform.[21]

H.R. 1504 further provides that the LEC "shall make available such capacity as is requested by unaffiliated video program providers upon reasonable notice," although the LEC "shall not be required . . . to provide more than 75 percent of the equipped capacity of its video platform to unaffiliated video program providers."[22]

Such provisions are troubling for several reasons. First, they would severely handicap the LEC in competing with cable operators (including out-of-territory telephone companies) that are free of general obligations to provide nondiscriminatory access. Because the network can be operated more profitably with the operator free to discriminate, as

---

19. S. 1086, 103d Cong., 1st Sess., § 613(b)(1)(A) (1993).
20. H.R. 3636, 103d Cong., 1st Sess., § 652(a) (1993).
21. *Id.* § 653(a).
22. *Id.* § 654(a).

emphasized in Chapter 4 regarding video dialtone, cable operators have strenuously resisted being saddled with common-carrier burdens. Why encourage wireline competition and at the same time handicap the LECs with such burdens? Selecting the LECs for handicapping seems a particularly poor choice, given the competitive pressure they will face in seeking a video foothold. Even with full parity in regulatory treatment, the LECs would have great difficulty competing with entrenched cable operators, as explained in Chapter 3. If anticompetitive use of network bottlenecks is anywhere a threat, the threat is not with the LECs that start from a zero video market share but with today's cable operators that have a virtual monopoly hold of wireline video access.

Second, nondiscriminatory access will be difficult to enforce if the LEC is intent on giving its affiliated programmers preferential access. The measure of nondiscrimination is not simply a single price for access, to be compared with others, but a whole set of terms and conditions, including response to service requests, channel positioning, and quality of service. This situation is starkly reminiscent of AT&T's predivestiture days. Recall that it was the difficulty of enforcing nondiscriminatory access toward unaffiliated interexchange carriers that led to separation of the BOCs from AT&T's interexchange service.

A better safeguard is a strong limitation on horizontal concentration. Not only is this measure more easily enforced, it gets directly to the problem by undermining the ability of the LEC to gain dominance in the program market through discrimination against nonaffiliated programmers.

Third, to the extent that nondiscrimination is successfully enforced, the outcome would weaken the economic benefits that the LEC (and ultimately society) would enjoy from vertical integration. As widely recognized in the Commission's decision and elsewhere, vertical integration reduces transaction costs between links in the production and distribution process, thereby enabling price reductions to consumers and, more generally, increasing economic efficiency. Among the benefits, vertical integration may facilitate production of programs that otherwise would not appear.[23]

These same benefits of vertical integration encourage preferences

23. *Horizontal and Vertical Ownership Limits, supra* note 5, at 8568-69 ¶ 7.

toward affiliated program suppliers. To illustrate, suppose that carrier *C* accommodates three independent program suppliers *X*, *Y*, and *Z*. Subsequently, *C* vertically integrates with *Y* to reduce transactions costs. Because dealings with *Y* involve lower costs than before, *C* would show a preference for *Y*—but only because the costs of dealing with *Y* are lower than without vertical integration, not because of any anticompetitive intent against *X* and *Z*. If *C* is prohibited from showing a preference toward *Y*, it would have weaker incentives to integrate with *Y* because the prohibition would make more difficult the capture of the benefits from integrating.

Econometric studies typically show that cable operators exhibit some preference, though not an overwhelming one, toward their program affiliates.[24] We would expect such an outcome as a reflection of economic efficiency. At the same time, the preferences identified in the studies could be also symptomatic of anticompetitive behavior. The two alternative hypotheses in these studies cannot be disentangled.

Measures taken to eliminate the preferences because of fears of anticompetitive conduct would have detrimental effects on vertical integration. The better course of action is to continue to permit firms to act upon their preferences for vertical integration but to adopt other measures (limitations on horizontal integration) to forestall anticompetitive effects.

Across-the-Board Common Carriage. So far we have considered parity in terms of granting the LECs the same non–common-carrier freedoms enjoyed by cable operators. But parity could be achieved in the other direction: impose common-carrier requirements on both the LECs and cable operators. Moving in that direction, H.R. 3636 would require the FCC to conduct a study of whether imposing common-carrier obligations also on cable operators would serve the public

---

24. BENJAMIN KLEIN, THE COMPETITIVE CONSEQUENCES OF VERTICAL INTEGRATION IN THE CABLE INDUSTRY (UCLA Working Paper 1989) (attachment to National Cable Television Association, Comments, MM Dkt. No. 92-264, Feb. 9, 1993); DAVID H. WATERMAN & ANDREW A. WEISS, THE EFFECTS OF VERTICAL INTEGRATION BETWEEN CABLE TELEVISION SYSTEMS AND PAY CABLE NETWORKS (Annenberg Sch. for Communication and Dep't of Economics, Univ. of S. Cal. Working Paper 1993); DAVID H. WATERMAN & ANDREW H. WEISS, VERTICAL INTEGRATION IN CABLE TELEVISION (Am. Enterprise Inst. Working Paper, 1993).

interest.[25]

Were the nation to start *de novo*, with no telecommunications infrastructure—or entrenched interests—in place, the establishment of a broadband common-carrier platform might be feasible. But at this stage of telecommunications development, the struggle to change course would be a long and perhaps impossible task. The early 1970s saw the high-water mark of public interest in cable common carriage.[26] Whatever battle was mounted, however, was quickly lost, save for a few commercial leased-access channels, as earlier discussed.

Moreover, it is not clear whether the struggle would be worth waging even if it ended in a common-carrier victory. As we concluded in Chapter 4, common carriage does not necessarily increase programming diversity. Moreover, with or without common carriage, the American public will have greater diversity of choice as channel capacities multiply. Greater competition in the multichannel marketplace, stemming from wireless technologies considered in later chapters as well as from wireline, will further increase program diversity even if none of the channel providers operates as a common carrier.

Prohibitions Against Local Buyouts

It is widely held that, with removal of the cross-ownership ban, telephone companies generally should not be permitted to buy out cable systems in their operating territories, since doing so would foreclose possibilities of competition between the two. As Representative Edward J. Markey, Chairman of the House Telecommunications Subcommittee, emphasizes, "A buyout, in which one monopolist is replaced by another monopolist, accomplishes nothing."[27]

For this reason, pending legislation would generally prohibit such acquisitions.[28] This policy of separation seems, in the near term, a

25. H.R. 3636, 103d Cong., 1st Sess., § 653(b) (1993).

26. *See* CABINET COMMITTEE ON COMMUNICATIONS, CABLE: REPORT TO THE PRESIDENT (1974); COMMITTEE FOR ECONOMIC DEVELOPMENT, BROADCASTING AND CABLE TELEVISION (1975); SLOAN COMMISSION ON CABLE COMMUNICATIONS, ON THE CABLE (McGraw-Hill 1971).

27. Rep. Edward J. Markey, Chairman, House Subcomm. on Telecommunications and Finance, Remarks Before the United States Telephone Ass'n 6 (Oct. 4, 1993).

28. *See* S. 1086, 103d. Cong., 1st Sess., § 656(a) (1993).

way to keep options open for wireline competition. In the longer term, however, the policy may pose serious dilemmas. Suppose that continuing technological advance tilts outcomes in favor of the single video wireline. Perhaps the optimal long-term solution would involve one entity supplying telephone service, another supplying video service, with the two sharing many elements of a single network—and both facing competition from wireless telephone and video operators. Perhaps a single network owned and operated by one entity would be an even better solution. But if these characteristics describe the most efficient production technology in the future, how could we harness that production technology with buyout prohibitions on the statute books?

To illustrate, suppose that competition between a LEC and incumbent cable operators emerges in the near term, perhaps with the LEC using ADSL technologies to permit use of its existing copper network for video. Suppose further that, in the longer term, construction of a single network is a better solution, given technological advances and evolving consumer needs. Achieving the single network might best be accomplished if one entity simply buys out the other or if they enter a joint ownership arrangement. Such arrangements would be facilitated if appropriate waivers to buyout prohibitions were available. H.R. 3636 specifies, for example, that buyouts are to be permitted if the cable system or systems in question "serve less than 10 percent of the households in the telephone service area" of the LEC or if the incumbent cable operator would be "subject to undue economic distress" or "would not be economically viable" with the enforcement of buyout prohibitions.[29]

Many situations may arise, however, that involve no clear economic distress or outright economic nonviability. Rather, the situation may involve two reasonably healthy entities that would be even healthier, and with significant cost savings flowing to society, if they were to merge or otherwise to engage in cooperative activities.

For now, prohibitions against buyouts, with waivers as written in pending legislation, are probably the best that can be expected. Yet, we must anticipate dilemmas in weighing the potential benefits of video

---

29. H.R. 3636, 103d Cong., 1st Sess., §§ 656(b)(2), (c)(1)(A) (1993).

competition (which may or may not emerge) against the benefits of in-territory LEC–cable cooperation or merger. Issues of delineating permissible relations between LECs and incumbent cable operators, based on experience yet to unfold, will occupy the attention of policy makers and others for a long time.

Information Diversity

We earlier suggested the possibility that subsidies from telephone ratepayers would not necessarily be used for anticompetitive price-cutting, but might be devoted to improving the range and quality of programming. Beyond issues of subsidies, the more general question arises about the effects on diversity of LEC involvement in programming. At first blush, it would seem easy to conclude that the LECs, by bringing additional financial resources to program production, would surely contribute to greater diversity.

One might counter, however, that if the LECs were merely to displace other players, the total financial base for programming would not expand. Others may observe that if a specific program is worth producing (that is, its expected revenues are greater than expected costs), the potential for profit will attract one entity or another for financial support, regardless of LEC participation.

Yet, it is reasonable to suppose that if the LECs succeed in gaining a video foothold against incumbent cable operators, they would not simply displace other players. It is also reasonable to believe that financial markets work only imperfectly: whether a particular opportunity is perceived as profitable enough to be worth seizing depends on the interests and financial capabilities of individual players. Adding the LECs to the group would widen both the interests and financial capabilities relevant to program production.

Without more detail here, we should consider the potentially positive effect of LEC involvement in programming. Among the questions we might contemplate are the following. If LEC entry increases the diversity of programming, would it be contrary to the Communications Act for the Commission not to permit such entry (to the extent that the agency has such discretion under the Act)? Would it violate the First

Amendment (on which the goal of program diversity supposedly is predicated) for Congress to forbid LEC entry into cable programming?

Regulatory Parity for Telephony

With the preceding emphasis on parity for LECs with cable operators for video services, it goes without saying that cable operators should be treated on a parity with the LECs in the provision of telephone services. Much has been written about the benefits of encouraging competition in local telephony, and there has been much speculation about the competitive effects of new technologies such as PCS services. As discussed earlier, inroads are being made by the CAPs, while cable operators are proceeding with field-tests and plans for commercial entry. Alliances between telephone companies and cable MSOs can be expected to strengthen the ability of cable systems to offer telephone service by virtue of skills contributed by out-of-territory telephone companies.

In general, the states have resisted the emergence of competition in local telephony because of its undesirable distributional effects.[30] As commonly said, the benefits to large businesses able to take advantage of competitive offerings are at the expense of residential and small business users who face higher rates than otherwise. This conflict highlights the long-standing and well-recognized need to ensure the continuation of universal service.

Fortunately, we may expect initiatives by more states toward open entry.[31] Among them, in late 1993 the California Public Utilities Commission sent to the governor a report that recommends action to "open all markets to competition and aggressively streamline regulation to accelerate the pace of innovation."[32]

An obvious possibility for accelerating the process is federal preemption of state authority to remove regulatory barriers to local compe-

---

30. For a summary of the regulatory framework in individual states, see NATIONAL ASS'N OF REGULATORY COMMISSIONERS, THE STATUS OF COMPETITION IN INTRASTATE TELECOMMUNICATIONS (1993).

31. Recent and planned sate initiatives are shown in *id.* at 165–67.

32. CALIFORNIA PUBLIC UTILITIES COMMISSION, ENHANCING CALIFORNIA'S COMPETITIVE STRENGTH: A STRATEGY FOR TELECOMMUNICATIONS INFRASTRUCTURE ix (1993).

tition.[33] Notably, H.R. 3636 stipulates that cable companies and other competitors are to be allowed equal access to, and interconnection with, local exchange facilities. Although detailed discussion goes beyond the scope of this study, such legislative thrusts deserve careful consideration.

Conclusions

The cross-ownership ban should be lifted if for no other reason than the ban is essentially irrelevant to commonly voiced concerns about potential anticompetitive behavior by the LECs. The only relevant distinction between LECs and cable operators is that the LECs have greater leeway to cross-subsidize by virtue of their captive telephone subscribers. If that threat is real, however, it results from transmission of video and telephone on the same network, not from LEC involvement in programming.

In its video dialtone decision, the Commission presumed that safeguards against cross-subsidization were adequate, but left the matter to later reassessment as the LECs proceed with their plans for the new service. The Commission should push ahead quickly with its reassessment, including especially the adequacy of its accounting rules and alternative remedial actions. As noted earlier, the rules, by requiring an allocation of common cost to video, provide a margin against underestimates of incremental costs. Among its many tasks, the Commission should determine the conditions under which this margin would play a significant role in protecting against cross-subsidization.

If safeguards against cross-subsidy are judged adequate to permit the LECs to provide video dialtone as defined under the FCC's current rules, no further concern is warranted on cross-subsidy grounds to letting the LECs also into video programming. Conversely, if the safeguards are judged inadequate, the FCC's decision to permit the LECs into video dialtone should be reversed. Or, more precisely, the LECs should be prohibited from offering video and telephone service on the same network—the source of the cross-subsidy threat.

33. For a detailed discussion of the division of power between the states and the federal government, see John R. Haring & Kathleen B. Levitz, *The Law and Economics of Federalism in Telecommunications*, 41 FED. COMM. L.J. 261, 262-330 (1989).

Any threat of anticompetitive use of local network bottlenecks is no more serious for the LECs than for today's cable operators. Indeed, to the extent that the threat exists at all, it is more serious for cable operators, which hold a virtual monopoly of video wireline service, while the LECs would start with a video market share of zero in seeking to compete with such powerful incumbents.

The appropriate safeguard against anticompetitive use of network bottlenecks is a regulatory limitation on horizontal concentration. The limitation already adopted by the Commission for cable could also be applied, if necessary, against the LECs for national programming. In cases where programming has only a regional or local audience, additional limitations on the LECs might be warranted because of their high level of local geographical concentration.

With the cross-ownership ban lifted, the LECs should be allowed to compete on full parity with cable operators. Especially, they should not be singled out for obligations to provide nondiscriminatory access to programmers or to discharge other common-carrier burdens because (1) these obligations would severely handicap the LECs in competing with cable operators who are free of such obligations, (2) the requirements would be troublesome and costly to enforce, and (3) to the extent that they are enforced, they would reduce the benefits that the LECs (and ultimately the public) would enjoy from integration into programming.

An alternative policy would achieve parity but from the other direction: impose common-carrier obligations on cable operators as well as on the LECs. As a practical matter, however, it would be difficult to turn back the clock to achieve a common-carrier–based cable industry. Moreover, the struggle to do so would probably not be worth winning. Common carriage does not necessarily increase programming diversity. In addition, with or without common carriage, the American public will have greater diversity of choice as channel capacities multiply. Competition in the multichannel marketplace, stemming from wireline technologies considered in later chapters as well as from wireline, will further increase program diversity even if none of the channel providers operates as a common carrier.

The widely supported approach of prohibiting LECs from buying out cable systems in their operating territories seems wise enough in the near term as a way to keep options open for wireline competition.

In the longer term, however, the policy may pose dilemmas in weighing the potential benefits of video competition (which may or may not emerge) against the benefits of in-territory LEC-cable cooperation or merger. Issues of delineating permissible relations between LECs and incumbent cable operators, based on information and experience yet to unfold, will occupy the attention of policy makers and others for a long time.

Finally, with the preceding emphasis on placing the LECs on regulatory parity with cable operators for video services, it goes without saying that cable operators should be treated on a parity with the LECs in the provision of telephone services. An obvious possibility for accelerating the process is federal preemption of state authority to remove regulatory barriers to local competition.

6

Satellite-Based Systems

THIS CHAPTER FOCUSES on the prospects for satellites to deliver multichannel video. With use of the geostationary orbit, where satellites placed 22,300 miles above the equator appear stationary, a single transmission beam can cover much or all of the nation. Two types of satellite service are relevant for our purposes. The first, direct broadcast satellite (DBS) service, provides video transmission directly to the viewer. The second, communications satellite service, provides video transmission to intermediate users—broadcasting stations and cable television systems that retransmit the signals to their viewers. A viewer with a suitable satellite receiver, a "home satellite dish," can, however, tune into these signals to bypass the intermediate link.

After reviewing the potential offered by DBS systems, we note the failed ventures of the early 1980s. Second, we treat the home satellite dish industry, which experienced rapid growth in the early 1980s until signal scrambling was introduced. Third, we examine the continuing development of more advanced systems incorporating video compression, aided by the ample spectrum space made available by the FCC for DBS systems. The chapter concludes with an assessment of the prospects for DBS systems to compete with cable.

Characteristics of Direct Broadcast Satellites

The salient characteristic of a DBS system, its nationwide or regional coverage from a single orbital location, gives a video provider great flexibility in entering (or exiting) particular local markets. The threat of price cutting by the incumbent cable operator has less force to deter DBS entry than is true of other multichannel systems. Against threatened entry by a second cable system or a LEC, an MSO could limit its price cutting to only the affected franchises. With the financial resources of its other franchises to draw on, the MSO, hoping to scare off a potential terrestrial entrant, could temporarily subsidize the affected franchises. In contrast, *all* the MSO's franchise areas are potentially at risk from DBS intrusion, rendering selective price cutting ineffective as a deterrent strategy. Thus,

> the DBS operator has greater flexibility than does a wireline operator. With the whole nation as a market, the DBS operator can draw from millions of potential subscribers. Unlike the case of wireline, the DBS operator does not need a large minimum penetration level in any given community to break even. Rather, the challenge is to aggregate enough subscribers across the nation to cover total cost.[1]

Against the attractions of wide signal coverage, DBS systems face three notable drawbacks. First, the upfront cost is high—hundreds of millions of dollars—for specially designed satellites dedicated to direct broadcasting. Not surprisingly, the need for such investment gives pause to venture capitalists. At the same time, the per-subscriber cost is low if even a small percentage of the nation's households sign up.

Second, the cost and aesthetics of the home satellite receiving equipment pose difficulties. The introduction of advanced satellites reduces the antenna size required for home installation from several feet to 18 inches. Nevertheless, the need for *any* such antenna is a handicap in competition with cable.

Third, at least for satellite designs being considered for the 1990s, DBS systems will not have the capacity to carry the signals of many local broadcasting stations or channels dedicated for use by individual subscribers. The same nationwide or regionwide coverage that makes DBS appealing also is an impediment. Even with the use of signal

---

1. Leland L. Johnson & Deborah R. Castleman, Direct Broadcast Satellites, A Competitive Alternative to Cable Television? 33 (RAND 1991).

compression to increase capacity, a DBS system could carry only a fraction of the more than 1,500 VHF and UHF local signals that are broadcast today.[2] Thus, conventional VHF-UHF antennas are needed by DBS subscribers—a drawback especially in areas of poor over-the-air reception.

This drawback could be remedied if, instead of regionwide or nationwide beams, narrower spot beams of 200 to 300 miles in diameter were used. One firm, Local DBS Inc., has proposed an approach that would allow DBS to carry all local broadcast signals within the area covered by the spot beam.[3] Such multiple narrow-beam satellites, however, would be more expensive than systems planned for operation within the next few years. If such satellites are shown to be technically and economically feasible, the time required for design and construction—after financing is in place—would probably delay their commercial use until the next century.

Early Ventures

Commercial DBS ventures, initiated in the early 1980s, were marked by failure. The most notable was the effort by the Communications Satellite Corporation (COMSAT) started in 1979 and abandoned in 1984—but only after COMSAT had ordered two satellites from RCA.[4] Other examples include (1) the United Satellite Communications, Inc., venture in which the Prudential Insurance Company reportedly lost nearly $70 million; (2) Skyband, Inc., which existed for only a few months at the expense of some $12 million; and (3) Crimson Satellite Associates, which after planning service on Satcom K-3 sold the satellite at a loss to a Luxembourg-based satellite broadcaster.[5] These

---

2. In addition to the 1,541 commercial and educational stations on the air as reported in BROADCASTING, May 10, 1993, at 55, construction permits were pending for 167 others. Moreover, 1,342 low-power VHF and UHF stations were in operation, some with signals carried on cable.

3. Local DBS Inc., Comments, MM Dkt. No. 93-25 (May 21, 1993).

4. As a consequence of its DBS venture, COMSAT took write-downs against revenues of $25 million and $120 million in 1984 and 1985, respectively. The $120 million figure amounted to 26 percent of COMSAT's total operating revenues for 1985 and was the dominant factor in its net loss of nearly $42 million reported for that year. COMSAT, 1984 SEC FORM 10-K, at 4 (1985).

5. BROADCASTING, Feb. 26, 1990, at 32.

attempts failed, in part, because of the need for large home antennas, the limited number of television channels offered, and difficulties in obtaining programming. COMSAT's plans, for example, called for three satellites, each with a capacity of only three channels.

Much has changed from these early days, as discussed below. More powerful satellites reduce the size of the receiving antennas, the use of digital transmission with signal compression expands channel capacity, and access to programming is now a less serious problem.

The Home Satellite Dish Market

Another factor that contributed to the defeat of early DBS ventures was the emergence of home satellite dishes (HSDs). These dishes, also called television receive only (TVRO) terminals, enable households to tune into satellite signals (transmitted in the C-band radio frequencies) that carry programming to broadcasting stations and cable systems.[6] By the early 1980s, the cost of satellite terminals for cable headends had fallen to the point where they became within reach of individual households. The antennas exceeded 6 feet in diameter and, with associated equipment, cost $3,000 or more. But the investment was attractive because it permitted direct access to the multitude of signals beamed to cable headends—without payment for the programs.

HSD sales grew rapidly during the early 1980s, illustrated in Figure 6-1. A sharp dropoff occurred, however, after signal scrambling was introduced in 1986. As described in one source, "A new era of satellite television dawned on January 15, 1986, when Home Box Office, Inc. began encrypting its satellite signal and then selling it to home satellite dish owners who had purchased a decoder. Other program services quickly followed HBO's example and began encrypting or 'scrambling' their satellite signals."[7] By the end of the decade, more than seventy-five signals available to HSD users were unscrambled and more than

---

6. The C-band frequencies are in the 4 GHz (4 billion hertz or cycles per second) to 6 GHz region of the spectrum.

7. Satellite Broadcasting and Communications Association, Comments, National Telecommunications and Information Administration, Dkt. No. 920532-2132 (1992).

FIGURE 6–1
ANNUAL SALES OF HOME SATELLITE DISH UNITS,
1980–93

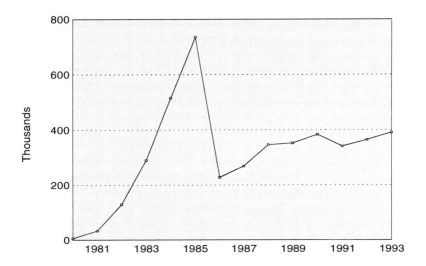

SOURCE: SATELLITE BROADCASTING AND COMMUNICATIONS ASS'N, SATELLITE TV 2 (undated).

thirty were scrambled. Not surprisingly, scrambled signals include pay channels and many of the most popular basic cable network services.[8]

By the end of 1993, the installed base of HSD terminals was about 4.4 million units, nearly 5 percent of the nation's 93 million television households.[9] HSD sales have been encouraged by (1) access to many dozens of television channels in addition to those carried by local cable systems, (2) the lack of cable service to several million house-holds, and (3) the pirating of scrambled signals through the illegal use of decoding systems.

8. *See* NATIONAL CABLE TELEVISION ASS'N, FACTS CONCERNING THE STATUS OF THE HOME SATELLITE DISH INDUSTRY AND SCRAMBLED PROGRAMMING 3 (Nov. 1989); unpublished data (on file with author).
9. SATELLITE BROADCASTING AND COMMUNICATIONS ASS'N, SATELLITE TV, at 2 (undated).

With respect to the last point, the first decoder used by the HSD industry, the VideoCipher II manufactured by General Instrument Corporation, was susceptible to signal pirating. According to one report, by 1990 more than 50 percent of the users of this decoder were not paying for programming.[10] A second version offering greater security, the VideoCipher II Plus, has fully replaced the earlier units. The DBS systems described below (Primestar and DSS) use encryption equipment from other manufacturers.[11]

Although the HSD market is continuing to grow, at least in part because of cable rate increases after the 1984 Cable Act was passed, this application of satellite technology will probably not play a major role in expanded competition with cable. The number of homes not passed by cable—the prime candidates for HSD service—has shrunk dramatically, from about 18 million households in 1984 to some 4 million in late 1992.[12] Moreover, as discussed below medium-power and high-power DBS systems offer lower-cost and less-obtrusive satellite receiving equipment. Retention of HSD terminals will be encouraged by the multitude of channels to which the HSD user will continue to have access in the C-band. In response to attractive DBS offerings, however, existing HSD owners will probably abandon their units if, over time, they require expensive maintenance or if aesthetics dictate a change to smaller antennas.

Satellite Master Antenna Television Systems

SMATV systems are essentially cable systems fed by HSD-type terminals to serve apartment buildings and other high-density dwellings.[13] These systems have lost market share, with subscribership dropping from 1 million in 1987 to ½ million in 1989.[14] This decline reflects,

10. Karen J. P. Hawes, *Encryption in the '90s*, VIA SATELLITE, June 1990, at 29.
11. For a description of encryption technology, see Inquiry into Encryption Technology for Satellite Cable Programming, PP Dkt. No. 92-234, 8 F.C.C. Rcd. 2925 (1993).
12. NATIONAL CABLE TELEVISION ASS'N, CABLE DEVELOPMENTS 1-A (June 1984); NATIONAL CABLE TELEVISION ASS'N, CABLE DEVELOPMENTS 1-A (Mar. 1993).
13. *See generally* FCC v. Beach Communications, Inc., 113 S. Ct. 2096 (1993).
14. Competition, Rate Deregulation and the Commission's Policies Relating to the Provision of Cable Television Service, Report, MM Dkt. No. 89-600, 5 F.C.C. Rcd. 4962, 5003 ¶ 69 (1990).

in part at least, the fact that some SMATV systems were built in areas that did not have cable service. Once cable service became available, the cable operators bought out the SMATV systems and integrated them into their own networks. As the cost of satellite receiving terminals continues to fall, SMATV systems will become more attractive.

Medium-Power Satellites

The preceding applications are based on low–power satellites that operate in the C-band radio frequencies allocated by the FCC for fixed satellite service (FSS).[15] In addition, a set of higher frequencies in the Ku-band is available for FSS.[16] This band is attractive for DBS use because it permits smaller receiving antennas than those needed at C-band frequencies. Operation at C-band frequencies requires a larger antenna to get the same size beam as at Ku-band frequencies because of the longer wavelengths of the C-band frequencies (at the expense, however, of greater susceptibility to rain fade—that is, signal loss caused by heavy rainfall).

Antenna size is dictated by two considerations: (1) the distances along the geostationary orbital arc of satellites that share the same radio frequencies and (2) the power density from the satellite at the ground (measured in watts per square meter). Regarding the first, the antenna must be large enough to discriminate between adjacent satellites. For operation within a given frequency band, the smaller the antenna, the wider its beam. For this reason, the minimum allowable antenna diameter is inversely related to the spacing of satellites that operate in the same frequency band. One handicap in using the FSS bands (both C-band and Ku-band) is that satellites are spaced closely together—only 2 degrees apart—along the orbital arc. The antenna size required to discriminate between satellites would be smaller if satellite spacing were widened. Regarding power density, the satellite is limited to no more than medium power (about 50 watts per transponder) because, with only a 2-degree spacing between satellites, the use of more power

---

15. The FSS band is intended for use by satellite receiving terminals that are fixed rather than mobile (such as on ships).

16. The Ku-band is in the frequency range of 12 GHz to 14 GHz, compared with the 4 GHz to 6 GHz range of the C-band.

would be wasteful: the smaller antenna that the added power would permit would be too small to discriminate among satellites spaced so closely together.[17] Despite the 2-degree satellite spacing, the FSS Ku-band is attractive for DBS use because satellites are already in use in that band for data, voice, and video applications and because transponders can be leased on attractive terms by DBS providers.

Taking advantage of low upfront costs by sharing satellite capacity with other users, K Prime Partners (now called Primestar Partners) placed a medium-power DBS system in operation in late 1990.[18] Investment is underwritten by six cable MSOs (including TCI) that account for nearly 50 percent of the nation's cable subscribers, together with satellite operator GE American Communications. The group is using an existing medium-power satellite (GE's Satcom K1) with ten transponders in the FSS band. The power of Satcom K1 and the 2-degree orbital spacing in the FSS band limit the minimum size of the receive antenna diameter to 3 feet.[19] The service uses analog instead of digital transmission and does not use compression techniques to multiply the number of channels. Thus, ten satellite transponders permit a capacity of ten full-time television channels.

Primestar equipment is provided to the subscriber along with the programming for a monthly subscription of $25 to $30 per month plus pay-per-view (PPV) charges. Primestar services are marketed by cable system operators, typically in unwired areas within the operator's franchise area.[20] Thus, Primestar is not generally offered in direct competition with cable. As of August 1993, Primestar had signed up 60,000 subscribers.[21]

Also in mid-1993, Primestar Partners announced a procurement of 500,000 consumer receivers for compressed signal delivery. This up

---

17. For a technical discussion, see H. Taylor Howard, *C-Band Antennas in a 2 Degree Spacing Environment*, 1991 WORLD SATELLITE ANNUAL 4-1 to 4-12 (Mark Long Enterprises 1991).

18. Sean Scully, *Primestar Buys Compression for $250M*, BROADCASTING & CABLE, Aug. 9, 1993, at 49.

19. BROADCASTING, July 30, 1990, at 38, 42.

20. Implementation of Sections of the Cable Television Consumer Protection and Competition Act of 1992, Rate Regulation, Report and Order, and Further Notice of Proposed Rulemaking, MM Dkt. No. 92-266, 8 F.C.C. Rcd. 5631, 5660 n.100 (1993).

21. Scully, *supra* note 18.

grade, scheduled for completion in 1994, would increase capacity to seventy channels or more.[22]

High-Power Satellites

Although the C-band and Ku-band are being used for residential satellite service, the attraction of wider satellite spacing—to permit smaller ground antennas—has persisted since the early DBS ventures. In response to urgings by DBS proponents, the FCC has allocated additional spectrum within a portion of the Ku-band known as the broadcast-satellite service (BSS) band. In accordance with international agreements, eight U.S. orbital positions have been established, each with the full BSS band. Most notably, the minimum satellite spacing was set at 9 degrees, in contrast to the 2–degree spacing in the FSS Ku-band. Each orbital position is allowed thirty-two transponder channels and a 24 MHz bandwidth per transponder.[23] Three of these eight positions enable full coverage of forty-eight states in the contiguous United States (CONUS). The others cover either the eastern or western portions of the United States.

A number of entities have been conditionally granted transponder channel positions in the BSS band (see Table 6–1). The grantees are in various planning stages for their systems. There is no assurance that all, or even many, of these systems will proceed as proposed to the FCC. Indeed, if past failures are any guide, we will witness many revisions in plans and eventual abandonments.

Table 6–2 summarizes the key characteristic of the low-, medium-, and high-power systems in operation or being planning. Especially noteworthy is the relationship between satellite power and receiving antenna diameter.

The high-power DBS system most advanced in planning and operation is the "Digital Satellite System" (DSS) sponsored by Hughes

---

22. *Id.*
23. Inquiry into the Development of Regulatory Policy in Regard to Direct Broadcast Satellites, Report and Order, Gen. Dkt. No. 80-603, 90 F.C.C. 2d 676 (1983). For a description of the technical aspects of these orbital assignments, see JOHNSON & CASTLEMAN, *supra* note 1, at 48–50.

TABLE 6–1
CONDITIONAL CONSTRUCTION GRANTS FOR DIRECT BROADCAST
SATELLITE SYSTEMS, 1992

Grantee	Channel Pairs
Advanced Communications Corp.	27
Continental Satellite Corp.	11
Direct Broadcast Satellite Corp.	11
Directsat Corp.	11
Dominion Video Satellite, Inc.	8
EchoStar Satellite Corp.	11
Hughes Communications, Inc.	27
Tempo Satellite Inc.	11
United States Satellite Broadcasting	8

NOTE: A channel pair has one transponder channel at one of the four eastern satellite locations and one at one of the four western satellite locations. Thus, all grantees are afforded full CONUS coverage with their channel pairs. These assignments were made in accordance with the FCC's evaluation of the merits of applications from potential DBS operators. The grants are conditional on the holder's demonstration of financial capability and other requirements on a time schedule established by the FCC.
SOURCE: Inquiry into the Development of Regulatory Policy in Regard to Direct Broadcast Satellites, Report and Order, Gen. Dkt. No. 80-603, 90 F.C.C.2d 676 (1983); *see also* G. WALL, R. POIRIER & A. BOUCHER, THE DBS REPORT 10 (Canadian Cable Television Ass'n 1992).

Communications. Two satellites with sixteen transponders each are to operate at 101 degrees west longitude, one of the three orbital slots visible from the entire CONUS, as noted earlier. Five transponders on the first satellite have been purchased by United States Satellite Broadcasting (USSB), listed in Table 6–2, for its own programming services, while eleven transponders on the first satellite and all sixteen trans-

TABLE 6–2

CHARACTERISTICS OF DIRECT BROADCAST SATELLITE SYSTEMS

DBS Power	Spectrum Use	Transponder Power	Receiving Antenna Diameter	Users
Low	C-band-FSS	2–15 watts	8–10 feet	Broadcasters, cable programmers
Medium	Ku-FSS	20–60 watts	3–4 feet	Primestar Partners
High	Ku-BSS	100–200 watts	1–2 feet	Nine FCC grantees

SOURCE: Adapted from WALL, POIRIER & BOUCHER, *supra* tab. 6–1, at 3.

ponders on the second will be operated by Hughes for its DirectTV service.[24] Using digital compression, the two-satellite system is to carry about 150 programming services. The first satellite was launched in December 1993, with commercial service planned for the spring of 1994.[25]

In addition, Primestar Partners may move into high-power DBS service through the acquisition of the DBS license held by Tempo Satellite (a subsidiary of cable operator TCI), listed in Table 6–1.[26] In turn, Tempo has awarded a $400 million contract to Space Systems/Loral for two satellites. Each satellite will have thirty-two transponders suitable for medium-power use but switchable to sixteen higher power transponders "that are optimized for digital broadcast service to cable heads and home satellite dishes using video compres-

24. Hughes Comm., *USSB Signs with Hughes for High-Power DBS Satellite Transponders*, Press Release, June 3, 1991, at 1.
25. Rich Brown, *Thomson Homes in on DBS Marketing*, BROADCASTING & CABLE, Dec. 20, 1993, at 59.
26. Scully, *supra* note 18.

sion to permit many broadcast channels per transponder."[27] Thus, Primestar Partners has the option of gearing the satellites for medium-power replacements of its current satellite use or for high-power use to compete directly with the Hughes/USSB system.

System Investment Costs. In contrast to medium-power satellite systems, high–power DBS systems, such as the one constructed by Hughes, require a large "space-segment" cost—approaching a billion dollars for satellites, launch, insurance, and signal uplink facilities.[28] At the same time, the smaller receiving antennas reduce manufacturing costs, facilitate installation, and reduce the negative aesthetic characteristics of residential outdoor receivers.

The per-subscriber satellite cost will depend on the number of households willing to subscribe. According to an earlier study, to amortize the space-segment cost of a high-power DBS system would involve an annual per-subscriber space segment charge of only $40 if 5 million households subscribed. But the figure would skyrocket to $400 if only 500,000 subscribed.[29] Thus, of key importance is the attainment of sufficiently low household satellite receiver costs (along with operating, programming, and other costs) to attract a large enough subscriber base against which the large investment in satellites can be spread.

The Hughes/USSB system consists of a set-top decoder and an 18–inch–diameter antenna, manufactured by Thomson Consumer Electronics. Thomson is to license manufacturing to others after eighteen months or after sales of 1 million units.[30] Initially, the receiving system for a single TV set is to be sold to residential subscribers at $699,

27. Loral Corporation, *Space Systems/Loral Receives $400 Million Contract for Two Direct-to-Home Broadcast Satellites*, Press Release, July 26, 1993.

28. The up-front cost of the Hughes/USSB system is not publicly known. The cost of a "model" DBS system (with four rather than two high-power satellites), however, is estimated at $950 million, including $400 million for satellites, $280 million for launch, $120 million for insurance, and $150 million for the uplink facilities. JOHNSON & CASTLEMAN, *supra* note 1, at 22.

29. *Id.* at 21–24. The amortized cost is based on the $950 million total, with assumptions of a ten-year and twenty-year life, respectively, for electronic and nonelectronic equipment, a ten-year life for satellites, and a 17 percent discount rate to reflect the DBS operator's pretax cost of capital.

30. Hughes Comm., *Hughes Selects Thomson and News Datacom to Provide DirecTV Receiving System*, Press Release, Feb. 3, 1992, at 2.

plus an installation fee of perhaps $150. Dual-set models (which require a separate decoder for each TV set) are to sell at $899.[31]

Operating, Marketing, and Administrative Expenses. It is difficult to assess the recurring expenses for DBS systems or how they compare with those of cable. Recall the sample drawn from the experience of an MSO with its cable systems, shown in Table 3-1. There is no reason to believe that marketing expenses and per-subscriber general and administrative expenses (42 percent of the total in Table 3-1) would significantly differ between DBS systems and large cable systems. But, with no DBS experience to draw on, differences could arise for reasons we cannot foresee.

Uncertainties surround network operations and maintenance because these functions differ greatly between cable and DBS systems. The adjustment and replacement of line amplifiers and the repair of cable breaks, for example, have nothing in common with DBS requirements. For DBS systems, the primary costs are associated with operation of the business center and satellite feeder link along with maintenance of user terminals. We lack satisfactory estimates for these elements because they include new technologies, such as video compression, that are not yet in commercial DBS operation. Since network operations and maintenance account for only about 23 percent of the costs in Table 3-1, however, disparities between cable and satellite experience may have little effect.

Competition with Cable

In evaluating the above comparisons with cable, three differences in services must be noted. First, signals carried at high radio frequencies by Ku-band DBS systems are subject to fade during heavy rainstorms. This disadvantage will be at least partially offset by the uniformly superior reception quality afforded by DBS at all other times.

Second, DBS has service limitations, as well as advantages, from widespread geographical coverage. The constraints on carrying signals of local broadcasting stations were emphasized earlier. Moreover, on-demand video is not likely to be economic with DBS systems, at least

31. Brown, *supra* note 25.

during this decade. As channel capacity increases, individual programs can be reshown at shorter intervals to suit the convenience of individual viewers, as with cable systems. But full on-demand video, with a channel dedicated to the use of a single subscriber, would be infeasible when a satellite signal, intended for a single subscriber, is spewn over a whole national or regional area. It is not clear whether this is a serious drawback for DBS, because the market for on-demand video is itself so unclear. More important is the potential of satellites to carry a panoply of conventional television fare that has proven audience appeal.

Third, DBS systems will have an advantage in introducing HDTV, discussed in Chapter 7. The conversion of a DBS feeder link to HDTV will permit instantaneous widespread coverage by satellite. For this reason, the first HDTV signals widely available to households may be transmitted by DBS satellites. In contrast, broadcasting stations will require costly retrofits for HDTV use. Large urban stations will probably be the leaders in this conversion process. Because some cable systems will be more adaptable for HDTV use than others, retrofits of cable networks will probably proceed unevenly. Consequently, cable systems and broadcasting stations will provide only patchwork coverage for HDTV during its early years. Depending on the sales growth of HDTV receivers, the emergence of HDTV could provide an additional impetus to market penetration by DBS systems, and vice versa.

On balance, no reason exists to believe that per-subscriber programming or administrative costs will be significantly different for DBS systems than for cable. Of key importance is transmission cost, which, for DBS systems, is dominated by the cost of the home satellite receiver. The installed cost of this receiver, from $850 to more than $1000 in the near term, is by itself about the same as the investment cost for upgraded cable systems, as discussed in Chapter 3. Under these circumstances, DBS systems will initially appeal to those deeply dissatisfied with existing cable service. On this basis, enough sign-ups may be achieved, drawing from a nationwide market, to enable DBS systems to break even.

More extensive audience appeal, however, will depend on reductions in home receiver costs—all the more so to offset cable's advantage in carrying local broadcast signals. Continued technological advances and mass production economies may well afford dramatic cost reductions. If the retail price of receivers is reduced to, say, $300 to $400—the price of a good-quality VCR—DBS systems will enjoy strong prospects. In the longer term, the emergence of HDTV will give additional impetus to DBS development.

Conclusions

Aside from lacking the potential advantage of DBS systems in providing HDTV, cable operators with their upgraded networks will be able to offer everything that DBS applications can provide and more (for example, signals of local stations and on-demand video). Furthermore, the cable operator can do so without the need for *any* outdoor receiving antenna. Successful competition with cable will depend on the ability of DBS operators to undercut the prices charged by cable operators for those services that both offer. The prospects for DBS operators will heavily depend on the retail price of home satellite receiver units. If the price can be pushed down to about $300 to $400 in mass production, DBS systems with their widespread coverage from a single orbital position would offer strong competition to cable.

7

Terrestrial Wireless Systems

IN ADDITION TO SATELLITE-BASED SYSTEMS, multichannel video can be transmitted terrestrially by wireless means. Notable methods are (1) multichannel, multipoint distribution service (MMDS), or wireless cable; (2) local multipoint distribution service (LMDS), which operates at higher radio frequency ranges than wireless cable; and (3) local broadcasting stations, which with the application of digital video compression could be converted to multichannel carriers.

We conclude that

- Wireless cable is a strong candidate for competition with cable. Its growth has been hampered by limitations on the availability of spectrum. But adoption of signal-compression techniques, permitting a multiplication of channel capacity, will alleviate this problem later in the decade.

- LMDS, with planned spectrum assignments, will have substantial channel capacity even without use of signal compression. Being an experimental application in a little-used spectrum space, however, its potential for widespread adoption is difficult to assess.

- Local broadcasting stations could be converted to multichannel distribution if spectrum space now reserved for single channels of high-definition television (HDTV) were used instead for multiple channels of lower-resolution broadcasting. But this application would require redirection of FCC policy regarding HDTV and the role of local broadcasting—a revision that would require years of contentious decision making. Consequently, local broadcasters will become multichannel competitors to cable only in the next century, if at all.

Wireless Cable

Wireless cable is a multichannel video service that is similar to cable television in the type of programming it provides but different from cable in that it uses line-of-sight microwave radio channels (in the 2.1 GHz and 2.5 GHz bands) rather than wireline to transmit programming. Households equipped with special rooftop antennas and electronics equipment receive signals transmitted from a tower up to about 30 miles distant. The same programming received by cable headends via satellite can be made available to wireless operators with satellite receiving antennas linked to their tower sites.

The primary advantage of wireless cable over wireline systems lies in its relatively low cost and ease of reaching potential subscribers. With an investment of $1–2 million for the tower and associated electronics equipment, the wireless operator can reach thousands of households, depending on local topography and demographics. With the subscriber's rooftop antenna and associated equipment costing perhaps $300–400, the total investment per subscriber may amount to no more than $400–500[1]—less than the $700 or so investment per subscriber typically associated with cable systems.[2]

Without the need for access to public rights of way, the wireless operator does not face the delays, uncertainties, and financial obligations associated with the requirements for obtaining and operating under a local franchise. Moreover, the FCC has declared that wireless cable does not fall within the definition of a cable television system for any statutory or regulatory purpose, thereby exempting wireless cable from the provisions of the Cable Acts of 1984 and 1992.[3]

---

1. Charles Haddad, *Cable Industry Under Air Attack*, ATL. J., Nov. 26, 1993, at G4.
2. *See supra* Chapter 2, note 8, and accompanying text.
3. Definition of a Cable Television System, Report and Order, MM Dkt. No. 89-35, 5 F.C.C. Rcd. 7638, 7638 ¶ 5 (1990).

Another advantage of wireless cable is that, without the need for amplifiers and other cable components, wireless transmission generally provides excellent reception quality with high technical reliability.[4] In contrast, some cable subscribers complain that they can receive better signals over the air from local broadcasting stations than from cable.

The wireless cable industry has been growing rapidly, at 40 percent to 50 percent during 1991 and 1992, but from a low base.[5] By mid-1993, the industry counted about 500,000 subscribers, with some 141 systems in operation or under construction.[6] Reflecting relatively low investment costs and freedom from legal constraints, the success of wireless systems has depended on undercutting cable subscriber fees for comparable programming. Table 7–1 compares the rates for basic service packages in eight metropolitan areas. In addition, pay channels and pay-per-view channels are commonly offered by wireless operators as well as by their cable counterparts.

The greatest problem facing the industry is the limited number of channels in the radio frequency space made available by the FCC. At most, thirty-three channels are available in the largest fifty markets, and thirty-two in the smaller markets. Twenty of these channels, however, are assigned or reserved for educational users in the instructional television fixed service (ITFS). A leading use of ITFS channels involves interconnection of scattered campus locations in school and college districts. The wireless operator is dependent on leasing ITFS channels for expanding capacity beyond the twelve or thirteen channels for which the operator can be directly licensed.

Although wireless operators are generally successful in leasing ITFS channels, the situation is complicated by two factors. First, the FCC has imposed restrictions on the use of ITFS channels to forestall the diversion of these channels to noneducational uses. It emphasizes "the critical importance of education, and the significant role ITFS can

---

4. NORDBERG CAPITAL, INC., THIRD GENERATION TELEVISION 3 (Oct. 21, 1993).
5. *Id.* at 1.
6. Unpublished data from the Wireless Cable Television Ass'n (on file with author).

TABLE 7-1
MONTHLY SUBSCRIBER RATES FOR BASIC SERVICE,
SELECTED LOCATIONS, APRIL 1992
(dollars)

Location	Coaxial Cable	Cable	Percentage Difference
Austin	21.95	18.95	14
Bakersfield	21.00	14.95	29
Colorado Springs	21.00[a]	16.95	19
Oklahoma City	20.08	13.95	31
Orlando	22.00	11.95	45
Riverside–San Bernadino	19.00[a]	12.95	32
Sacramento	21.50	16.95	21
Tucson	23.00	16.00	30

a. Rates averaged in areas with multiple cable systems.
SOURCE: Unpublished data from the Wireless Cable Television Association.

play in providing improved educational opportunities for all."[7] It has restated its continuing commitment not to "jeopardize the current or future ability of ITFS to fulfill its primary intended purpose of providing educational material for instructional use."[8]

Accordingly, the Commission imposes restrictions on applications for channels reserved for ITFS. The ITFS licensee must provide no fewer than twenty hours per week per channel of ITFS programming before leasing any excess capacity. An additional twenty hours per week per

7. Amendment of Parts 21, 43, 74, 78, and 94 of the Commission's Rules Governing Use of the Frequencies in the 2.1 and 2.5 GHz Bands Affecting: Private Operational-Fixed Microwave Service, Multipoint Distribution Service, Multichannel Multipoint Distribution Service, Instructional Television Fixed Service, and Cable Television Relay Service, Second Report and Order, Gen. Dkt. No. 90-54, 6 F.C.C. Rcd. 6792, 6792 ¶ 1 (1991) [hereinafter *Wireless Cable Proceeding, Second Report and Order*].
8. *Id.*

channel must be "reserved for recapture by the ITFS licensee, during hours of the day and days of the week to be negotiated by the licensee and lessee."[9]

Second, these arrangements impose a cost burden on the wireless operator, which must arrange for proper location of transmitting antennas and other equipment required for shared channel use. Moreover, ITFS licensees generally charge lease fees that together may run to perhaps 5 percent of the wireless operator's gross revenues.[10]

Moreover, the growth of wireless cable has been slowed because of the FCC's time-consuming deliberations and cumbersome administrative procedures. A large backlog of applications for spectrum licenses is being reduced because of recent streamlining of these procedures. By early 1993, the Commission had issued more than 900 licenses.[11]

Under FCC rules, each transmitter is protected over only a 15-mile radius from signal interference from other spectrum users.[12] Thus, the location of some households may permit choices among competing wireless systems in addition to the service provided by an incumbent cable operator.

Use of Compression Technology. As with other delivery systems, the use of video compression techniques could markedly affect this industry's fortunes. With signal decoders added to subscribers' equipment to enable a channel multiplication of, say, four to one, the wireless cable operator would be able to offer as many as 132 channels within existing spectrum assignments.

---

9. Rules Governing Use of the Frequencies in the 2.1 and 2.5 GHz Bands, Order on Reconsideration, Gen. Dkt. Nos. 90-54, 80-113, 6 F.C.C. Rcd. 6764, 6774 ¶ 50 (1991). In setting down these rules, the FCC reemphasized its concern that "entities not primarily interested in providing ITFS programming" not become ITFS licensees. *Id.* at 6774 n.45.

10. NORDBERG CAPITAL, *supra* note 4, at 4.

11. Rulemaking to Amend Part 1 and Part 21 of the Commission's Rules to Redesignate the 27.5–29.5 GHz Frequency Band and to Establish Rules and Policies for Local Multipoint Distribution Service, Notice of Proposed Rulemaking, Order, Tentative Decision, and Order on Reconsideration, CC Dkt. No. 92-297, 8 F.C.C. Rcd. 557, 558 ¶ 18 (1993).

12. Some have argued that the radius should be increased—to 30 miles, for example. But as the FCC noted, "some petitioners were quite candid in acknowledging that their purpose in requesting our enlargement of the protected service area was to foreclose competition from a newcomer station." Order on Reconsideration, *supra* note 9, 6 F.C.C. Rcd. at 6765 ¶ 5.

Not surprisingly, strong interest is being expressed in exploiting the new technology; experiments are being conducted to test performance with existing wireless systems. The nation's five largest wireless cable operators are contributing $1 million to fund development of digital compression and interactive technology tailored to use in the 2 GHz spectrum band.[13] The new organization—the Wireless Cable Research and Development Center—will draw support from more than a dozen hardware suppliers.[14]

The use of video compression offers several possibilities to wireless operators: (1) to continue to offer more limited programming than available through high-capacity cable systems but at a lower subscriber price than charged for comparable cable packages; (2) to compress all signals, with households desiring service required to add decompression equipment; and (3) to transmit uncompressed signals on some channels and compressed signals on the remainder to give households the choice of inexpensive limited service with uncompressed signals or more costly service with a combination of compressed and uncompressed signals. Whether the industry moves in one direction, or whether all three options will be pursued, will depend largely on the costs of decoders and local demographics. In any event, three to five years may be required to convert the wireless cable industry to compressed signal transmission.[15] The Commission is investigating ways in which, during the interim, wireless cable operators and ITFS channel licensees might cooperate in scheduling channel use to enhance the effectiveness of leased channels for commercial purposes while not compromising the roles and responsibilities of ITFS users.[16]

Future Prospects. With the relatively low cost and ease with which wireless systems can be installed, we can reasonably expect wireless cable to thrive in many markets that have good line-of-sight characteristics. Hills, trees, buildings, and other obstructions create shadow areas, which limit available service areas. In some cases, signal boost-

13. BROADCASTING & CABLE, Apr. 26, 1993, at 80.
14. Wireless Cable Ass'n Int'l, Comments, MM Dkt. No. 93-106, at 8–9 (June 14, 1993).
15. *Id.* at 9.
16. Amendment of Part 74 of the Commission's Rules Governing Use of the Frequencies in the Instructional Television Fixed Service, Notice of Proposed Rulemaking, MM Dkt. No. 93-106, 8 F.C.C. Rcd. 2828 (1993).

ers can be used to receive the signal from one direction and to redirect it in another to reach areas inaccessible from the main transmitter. But the additional costs involved, along with limitations imposed by the need to avoid signal interference, render signal boosters only a partial remedy.

DBS is a close competitor to wireless cable. In this race, wireless cable has one major advantage. With the limited geographical coverage afforded from a transmitter, wireless cable operators can more readily carry the signals of local broadcasting stations. The impact of this advantage will depend on the quality of over-the-air reception in the locality in question.

Wireless operators face two notable disadvantages relative to DBS systems. First, because of low antenna elevation angles, more of their potential markets are in shadow areas. If the transmitter tower is 500 feet tall, a home antenna 10 miles away has less than a ½–degree elevation angle. In contrast, a satellite in geosynchronous orbit enables a much steeper viewing angle (the precise angle being determined by the satellite's orbital position and the user's geographical location). From a satellite located, for example, at 110 degrees west longitude—one of the eight orbital position designated for domestic DBS service—ground antenna elevation angles range from about 25 degrees to 55 degrees over the entire contiguous United States.

Second, limited spectrum resources will continue to be a problem. The thirty-two channels available to wireless cable in most local markets is the same number available at each of the eight orbital slots assigned to DBS. But many wireless channels will continue to be encumbered by ITFS responsibilities, limiting their availability to meet the interests of the general public. These limitations may make it difficult for the wireless cable operator to exploit fully the advantage over DBS in carrying local broadcasting signals. The use of digitally compressed signals will expand capacity (at an additional cost), but for any given level of channel multiplication, more derived channels will be available from each orbital slot than can be provided by the wireless operator—depending on the degree of terrestrial channel encumbrance due to ITFS use in specific local markets.

A final point: to encourage competition, the FCC prohibits cross-ownership between cable and wireless cable operators in the same service territory.[17] Cable–wireless cable combinations that existed before early 1990 have been grandfathered in response to complaints, mainly by cable operators, that "divestiture would be unduly disruptive and would deprive customers of service."[18] Because grandfathering will cover only a small portion of the industry as it continues to grow, however, common ownership will pose only a slight impediment to competition. As discussed in Chapter 8, a more general cross-ownership restriction between wireless and wireline systems in the same geographical market would likely confer social benefits, in terms of encouraging competition, that outweigh any downside loss.

Local Multipoint Distribution Service

Historically, technological advances have greatly helped to alleviate congestion in spectrum use by enabling the exploitation of progressively higher frequencies. One recent example is broadband transmission at frequencies higher than the 2 GHz region available to wireless cable operators.

In early 1991, the FCC authorized Hye Crest Management, Inc., a wholly owned affiliate of the Suite 12 Group, to construct and operate a transmitter in the 28 GHz band for video service in Brighton Beach, a suburb of New York City.[19] With a capacity of forty-nine video channels in the 28 GHz region, the transmission facility was completed in mid-1992. Bell Atlantic has joined in a partnership with CellularVision of New York (affiliated with the Suite 12 Group) to operate the system and, with multiple transmitters, to offer the service within the five boroughs of New York City and in several adjacent counties.[20]

17. Amendment of Parts 21, 43, 74, and 94 of the Commission's Rules Governing Use of the Frequencies in the 2.1 and 2.5 GHz Bands Affecting: Private Operational-Fixed Microwave Service, Multipoint Distribution Service, Multichannel Multipoint Distribution Service, Instructional Television Fixed Service, and Cable Television Relay Service, Report and Order, Gen. Dkt. Nos. 90-54, 80-113, 5 F.C.C. Rcd. 6410, 6417 ¶ 42 (1990).
18. *Wireless Cable Proceeding, Second Report and Order, supra* note 7, 6 F.C.C. Rcd. at 6799 ¶ 38.
19. Hye Crest Management, Inc., File No. 10380-CF-P-88, 6 F.C.C. Rcd. 332 (1991).
20. CellularVision of New York, *CellularVision of New York in Partnership with Bell Atlantic to Roll-Out Alternative Cable Service in New York*, Press Release, Aug. 4, 1993.

After granting the authorization to Hye Crest, the FCC received 971 applications from entities elsewhere in the nation to provide service similar to that of Hye Crest.[21] In response to petitions for an FCC rulemaking on proposed uses for the 28 GHz band, the Commission issued a notice of proposed rule making in early 1993. It proposed to establish a new "local multipoint distribution service" (LMDS) in the 27.5–29.5 GHz frequency range.[22] The Commission contemplates division of 2,000 MHz into two 1,000 MHz blocks to be assigned to two competing licensees in each area—similar to the duopoly approach in cellular telephone service.[23] An LMDS system would use an omnidirectional antenna to transmit from the node, or center, of a cell. As with wireless cable, the subscriber would have a special receiver antenna aimed at the transmitter. With each cell 6 to 12 miles in diameter and with spectrum reuse among the cells, a number of cells would be required to cover a metropolitan area—a configuration familiar in cellular telephony.

Applications for a particular market are to be made in accordance with procedures to be established by the Commission. Winners will be selected either by a lottery or by auction.[24] Among the proposed requirements enforced on winners, service must be made available to 90 percent of the residents within the local service area within three years.[25] The Commission has initially proposed that both LECs and cable operators be eligible for LMDS licenses but leaves resolution of cross-ownership issues open for later determination.[26] At this writing, the Commission has received comments on its proposals but has yet to make final decisions.

21. Rulemaking to Amend Part 1 and Part 21 of the Commission's Rules to Redesignate the 27.5–29.5 GHz Frequency Band and to Establish Rules and Policies for Local Multipoint Distribution Service, Notice of Proposed Rulemaking, Order, Tentative Decision and Order on Reconsideration, CC Dkt. No. 92-297, 8 F.C.C. Rcd. 557, 558 ¶ 6 (1993) [hereinafter *Local Multipoint Distribution Service*].
22. *Id.* at ¶ 20.
23. Local service areas are synonymous with Basic Trading Areas as defined in the Rand McNally *1992 Commercial Atlas and Marketing Guide*, plus Alaska and Puerto Rico, for a total of 489 areas. *Id.* at ¶ 30.
24. *Id.* at ¶ 36.
25. *Id.* at ¶ 47, 48.
26. *Id.* at ¶ 33.

Here, as elsewhere, the Commission is motivated by its desire to promote multichannel video competition. It concludes that "the 28 GHz band is virtually unused, and the proposals before us, if developed to their apparent potential, will provide consumers with additional options by which to satisfy video and other telecommunications options."[27] It observes that "a new source of competition for franchised cable companies, wireless cable companies, and other video service providers furthers our goal of using the disciplines of the marketplace to regulate the price, type, quality and quantity of video services available to the public."[28]

LMDS has an advantage over wireless cable with its greater capacity—perhaps some forty-nine unencumbered channels in each of two bands. This capacity affords a wide variety of video and two-way interactive services—all the more so with applications of digital signal compression. It also shares the disadvantage of spotty signal coverage, dictated by line-of-sight reception requirements and low antenna angles.

LMDS has another notable disadvantage. With the more limited coverage per transmitter, the cost of covering a metropolitan area will be higher than that for wireless cable.

It is difficult to predict the future of LMDS because of technical uncertainties that will be resolved only after further experimentation and early commercial experience. Two factors are noteworthy. First, transmission is more susceptible to rain fade—signal loss caused by heavy rainstorms—at 28 GHz than at lower wireless cable frequencies. Whether the smaller cell size and shorter transmission distances at 28 GHz can contain this problem will be known only when propagation characteristics at such high frequencies become better understood.

Second, the success of LMDS depends critically on the sharing of frequencies between adjacent cells. Differences in transmission characteristics and directional discrimination afforded by subscribers' receiving antennas will be relied on to avoid interference between cells. Whether these protections will suffice remains to be seen, especially since widely varying topographical characteristics and weather conditions may contribute to interference problems.

---

27. *Id.* at 558 ¶ 3.
28. *Id.* at 559 ¶ 16.

All in all, if use of the 28 GHz band proves technically and economically feasible, LMDS could prove a strong competitor to both wireline and other wireless systems. Indeed, with the capacity afforded by LMDS, the movement of wireless cable out of the congested 2 GHz band might be merited as a way to free these spectrum resources for more highly valued uses. Such a move would be preceded by long and painful controversy, extending into the next century.

Local Broadcasting Stations

With so much public focus on multichannel television, it is easy to lose sight of the importance of broadcasting. Although the number of local stations has played a key role in the FCC's definition of effective competition, Congress dropped all reference to the number of stations in its definition, as discussed in Chapter 1. It concluded that the presence of effective competition by broadcasting—or by any other source—would be adequately identified if a cable subscriber penetration rate of less than 30 percent exists within the market in question. (But, to reiterate, a 30 percent threshold is a questionable criterion for judging the effectiveness of competition.)

Two scenarios merit assessment: (1) continuation of single-channel, advertiser-supported programming and (2) conversion from single-channel to multichannel operation through the use of video compression. The key common element of these alternatives is the continued use of today's allocations (below 1 GHz) of spectrum space for television broadcasting—in contrast to the use of higher frequencies for wireless cable and LMDS.

Single Channel, Advertiser Support. Under this scenario, broadcasters continue in essentially today's operating mode. Predictions are commonplace that broadcasting, faced by expanding competition from cable and other multichannel providers, will play a diminishing role in American society. As one example, a comprehensive FCC study concludes:

Broadcast television . . . . has suffered an irreversible long-term decline in audience and revenue share, which will continue throughout the current decade . . . . Although broadcasting will

TABLE 7-2
ALL-DAY VIEWING SHARES, CABLE AND NONCABLE
HOUSEHOLDS, 1984–85 AND 1989–90
(Percent)

Program Source	Cable Households		Non-Cable Households	
	1984–85	1989–90	1984–85	1989–90
Network Affiliates	53	43	74	70
Independents	20	15	22	24
Cable Programming	24	39	—	—

SOURCE: SETZER & LEVY, *infra* note 29, at 23.

remain an important component of the video mix, small-market stations, weak independents in larger markets, and UHF independents in general will find it particularly difficult to compete, and some are likely to go dark.[29]

Driving these conclusions are the facts that (1) the viewing share of broadcasting stations in cable households has declined in recent years, as shown in Table 7-2, and (2) profits as a percentage of revenue, particularly of network affiliates, have fallen.[30] Yet the number of broadcasting stations, especially UHF stations, shown in Table 7-3, continued to grow, while 164 construction permits for new stations were outstanding in early 1993.[31] Moreover, broadcast advertising revenues have continued to grow in real terms.[32]

29. FLORENCE SETZER & JONATHAN LEVY, BROADCAST TELEVISION IN A MULTICHANNEL MARKETPLACE vii (FCC Office of Plans & Policy Working Paper No. 26, 1991).
30. *Id.* at 37.
31. BROADCASTING & CABLE, Apr. 26, 1993, at 70.
32. SETZER & LEVY, *supra* note 29, at 41.

TABLE 7-3
NUMBER OF COMMERCIAL BROADCASTING STATIONS
ON THE AIR, 1975, 1990, AND 1992

	1975	1990	1992
VHF	514	547	558
UHF	192	546	588
Total	706	1,093	1,146

SOURCE: For 1975 and 1990, SETZER & LEVY, *supra* note 29, at 15; for 1992, BROAD-CASTING & CABLE, Apr. 26, 1993, at 70.

How can one explain these continued upward trends in light of the growth of cable and the burgeoning videocassette market, which inevitably cut into broadcaster audiences? In response, we must turn to a bit of history.

In the earliest days of cable, when it brought signals to areas without good access to local broadcasting stations, cable was generally seen as a valuable adjunct to broadcasting. By extending the range and improving the reception of locally broadcast signals, cable—or community antenna television (CATV)—expanded the audiences of broadcasters to the benefit of all.

But the situation changed during the 1960s and 1970s, when cable started bringing outside signals into areas already served by local stations. Concerns arose that advertising revenues of local stations would fall with the loss of audiences and that some stations would go off the air, thereby depriving viewers of "free" television.

The threat was seen as particularly serious for struggling UHF stations that were already handicapped in competing with VHF stations.[33] In making large amounts of radio spectrum available for UHF

33. These handicaps arose from the inferior propagation characteristics of UHF signals compared with VHF, the absence on early receivers of UHF tuners, the difficulty of using UHF tuners supplied with some receivers, and the poor quality of tuners supplied by some manufacturers. For a comprehensive discussion, see FCC OFFICE OF PLANS & POLICY, UHF COMPARABILITY TASK FORCE (Sept. 1980).

broadcasting, the FCC hoped that numerous UHF stations would emerge and add to the quantity and diversity of programming available to the American public. These hopes would be dashed, many argued, if UHF stations were faced with competition from signals imported by cable operators.[34]

Why were forebodings of the demise of free TV so wrong? Two factors were at work. First, audience fragmentation was offset by improved reception of locally broadcast signals (particularly important for UHF stations) and by the greater geographic coverage afforded by cable carriage. Second, some stations harmed by the fragmentation of their audience by imported signals were, in turn, carried into distant markets. Indeed, some stations—called "superstations"—tailor their programming and advertising appeal specifically to a nationwide market, with transmission of their signals relayed by satellite to distant cable headends.

An additional factor, becoming increasingly important, lies in opportunities for shared program costs between cable and over-the-air delivery. In the same way that cable was heavily dependent on the carriage of broadcast signals during cable's early days, broadcasters may become increasingly dependent on programming produced primarily for cable systems. With such shared use, which reduces the cost of programming that must be borne by broadcasters, we may well see a continued increase in the number of stations and emergence of additional broadcast networks. A race is already taking place between Paramount and Warner Brothers to form a fifth network, with each rushing to sign up affiliates.[35] We can expect more such efforts later in the decade and beyond.

More generally, it is reasonable to conjecture that broadcasting and cable will continue in a highly synergistic relationship but with a reversal of historical patterns. Where, in times past, cable operators depended heavily on programming carried by broadcasting stations, broadcasting stations will become increasingly dependent on programming carried on cable systems. A station may evolve to the point where it sim-

34. For a detailed account of these concerns in the late 1960s, see PRESIDENT'S TASK FORCE ON COMMUNICATIONS POLICY, FINAL REPORT (G.P.O. 1968).

35. Joe Flint, *Clash of the Titans, Fifth-Network Style*, BROADCASTING & CABLE, Dec. 20, 1993, at 38–39.

ply transmits over the air a cable channel or portions of several cable channels.

This synergistic relationship is most notable for our purposes. Large numbers of stations remaining on the air will provide a competitive check against the market power that can be exercised by cable or other multichannel systems. Recall that more than one-third of the households passed by cable do *not* subscribe. Millions of households prefer not to pay the $20, $30, or more per month for cable but opt for free television. Expressed differently, if all broadcast stations went off the air tomorrow, new sign-ups to cable would skyrocket. Although broadcasting is not as close a substitute for cable as other alternatives we have considered, its competitive role in the marketplace must not be ignored.

Multichannel Broadcasting, Advertiser-Viewer Support. Although single-channel advertiser-supported television may remain quite viable into the foreseeable future, broadcasters are anxious to share in the opportunities perceived in the technological revolution in telecommunications. One possibility is use of digital video compression to multiply channel capacity. With modifications at the station, a broadcaster could transmit several channels to viewers equipped with suitable decoders.

Where would the spectrum space be found for digital multichannel service? The quick answer is to divide the digital channels now planned for HDTV transmission into multiple compressed signals usable by today's NTSC receivers.[36] This possibility brings us to the FCC's plans for the development of HDTV, in which local broadcasters are to play a prominent role.

Japan and several Western European countries have devoted great effort to the development of HDTV, for which, in all cases, satellites are planned as the primary vehicle for signal transmission. Indeed, one hour of HDTV broadcasting daily is transmitted in Japan via satellite to the few (and expensive) HDTV receivers there.

---

36. The National Television System Committee, a committee of industry representatives, agreed to the NTSC standard for black-and-white broadcast television in 1940 and for color television in the early 1950s. The history of the Committee's deliberations is recorded in COLOR TELEVISION STANDARDS: SELECTED PAPERS AND RECORDS (Donald G. Fink ed., McGraw Hill 1955); TELEVISION STANDARDS AND PRACTICE: SELECTED PAPERS OF THE NATIONAL TELEVISION SYSTEM COMMITTEE AND ITS PANELS (Donald G. Fink ed., McGraw Hill 1943).

Although satellites and cable are recognized in the United States as obvious candidates for HDTV transmission, FCC policy has focused primarily on transmission of HDTV signals by today's local broadcasters. Consequently, much work has gone into perfecting signal compression techniques to squeeze an HDTV signal (requiring about five times the information rate of a conventional signal) into the 6 MHz bandwidth used for standard analog NTSC broadcasting.

The FCC expressed interest in HDTV (or advanced television, as it is also known) in 1987, when it launched an inquiry into relevant technical, economic, legal, and policy issues. It also established the Advisory Committee for Advanced Television Service to assist the Commission in making its decisions.[37]

After examining filings of interested parties and the recommendations of the Advisory Committee, the FCC has decided that any advanced television program transmitted by a broadcasting station must be receivable on existing sets. That is, the receiver must be able to display the program (without a special converter) at a quality comparable to that provided by the NTSC standard. The FCC subsequently decided that the best way to attain this compatibility is to use a simulcast mode. Each incumbent broadcaster is to be assigned an HDTV channel, which will be programmed by the broadcaster alongside its existing analog NTSC channel.[38] Households with conventional NTSC receivers will continue to be served as today, while those with HDTV receivers will tune to the new channel. After a sufficient percentage of households has converted to HDTV, presumably early in the next century, NTSC service is to be phased out, and the freed spectrum space is to be made available for other uses.

---

37. Advanced Television Systems and Their Impact on the Existing Television Broadcast Service, Tentative Decision, and Further Notice of Inquiry, MM Dkt. No. 87-268, 3 F.C.C. Rcd. 6520 (1988).

38. Advanced Television Systems and Their Impact on the Existing Television Broadcast Service, Memorandum Opinion and Order, Third Report and Order, and Third Further Notice of Proposed Rulemaking, MM Dkt. No. 87-268, 7 F.C.C. Rcd. 6924 (1992) [hereinafter *Advanced Television Third Report and Order*]. For a scathing critique of the FCC's plan to grant HDTV licenses only to existing broadcasters, see Bob Davis, *FCC to Grant Owner of Every TV Station Another License Free*, WALL ST. J., Mar. 19, 1992, at A1.

This FCC-supported effort must be regarded as a most impressive technical achievement. Early in the Commission's deliberations, analog transmission was generally thought the leading contender for HDTV use because serious difficulties were associated with digital techniques. Notably, the HDTV transmission standards developed in Japan and being used there today and the standards proposed by Japan's NHK in the late 1980s for use in the United States are based on analog transmission.[39]

In a formal testing program overseen by the FCC's Advisory Committee, competing approaches to HDTV transmission have been evaluated. In 1990, during the Commission's test planning, General Instrument announced development of its all-digital DigiCipher to be offered for FCC evaluation. Soon thereafter, the other leading contenders (except NHK) modified their proposals to incorporate digital transmission. After testing of five systems was completed in early 1993, no one system was judged as the clear winner. Although NHK's analog entry was discarded as deficient, the other digital systems had varying mixtures of strengths and weaknesses. In response, the contenders agreed to combine forces to develop a single HDTV standard for FCC approval. This Grand Alliance, as it is called, combines the talents of AT&T, Zenith Electronics Corporation, General Instrument Corporation, the Massachusetts Institute of Technology, David Sarnoff Research Center, Philips Consumer Electronics, and Thomson Consumer Electronics.[40] In early 1994, the alliance announced its selection of the system proposed by Zenith for HDTV transmission for terrestrial broadcast and cable.[41]

Possibilities exist for a vast expansion of the information capacity of the nation's (indeed, the world's) spectrum resources. The development of digital video compression, whose potential applications are referenced throughout this study, was spurred in part by the FCC's HDTV program. A digital transmission system can be superimposed on an

39. LELAND L. JOHNSON, DEVELOPMENT OF HIGH DEFINITION TELEVISION: A STUDY IN U.S.-JAPAN TRADE RELATIONS (RAND June 1990).
40. Grand Alliance, *Digital HDTV Grand Alliance Makes Key Technology Decisions*, Press Release, Oct. 21, 1993.
41. Grand Alliance, *Digital HDTV Grand Alliance Selects Digital Transmission Technology*, Press Release, Feb. 16, 1994.

analog system, with less interference than would arise in a pure analog environment. This characteristic will permit existing broadcasters to transmit analog and digital signals simultaneously within existing spectrum allocations for broadcasting.

At the same time, the wisdom of the FCC's emphasis on transmission of HDTV by local broadcasters is questionable. The basic danger with the FCC's approach is that broadcasters will be using an enormous amount of spectrum for HDTV transmission to HDTV viewers, virtually none of whom will depend on local broadcasters for service. The viewers most likely to purchase HDTV receivers (which we must assume will cost substantially more than their NTSC counterparts) will be drawn from middle- and upper-income levels and lower-income viewers who enjoy watching a lot of television. These are precisely the people most likely to subscribe to cable, DBS, or other multichannel services.[42] Thus, the potentially large social benefits of digital transmission and signal compression threaten to be largely wasted with transmission of HDTV by local broadcasters to a small or virtually nonexistent over-the-air audience. Even if sales of HDTV receivers soar, few viewers will depend on over-the-air reception. HDTV broadcasters will serve essentially as programmers for cable and other multichannel systems.

One could counter that lower-income groups and others who do depend more heavily on over-the-air broadcasting will buy HDTV receivers as their prices fall over time. But this argument ignores the probability that prices of conventional NTSC receivers will also fall, as they have in the past, as a consequence of technological advance and more efficient manufacturing techniques. Into the foreseeable future, HDTV receivers, with their bigger screens and greater information processing requirements, will be more expensive than their NTSC counterparts. Consequently, a market is likely to persist for inexpensive NTSC receivers, primarily among low-income groups who value free over-the-air television. Thus, the FCC may face great difficulty in implementing its plans to phase out NTSC analog broadcasting early

---

42. A test of this proposition would involve determining how many purchasers of today's big screen NTSC receivers depend on over-the-air broadcasting for reception, rather than subscribing to cable or other multichannel service. Unfortunately, data on this point are not readily available.

in the next century and to assign the spectrum to more highly valued uses.

Conceivably, inexpensive converters could be developed to enable today's NTSC receivers to operate with HDTV signals (with reception comparable to that from NTSC signals). Use of such converters would help alleviate public pressures for continuation of analog broadcasting. But this outcome would be bizarre: broadcasters incur large costs for station equipment and other facilities to transmit digital HDTV signals only to force viewers to spend money to convert the signals to a lower resolution viewable on their non-HDTV receivers.

The situation is further complicated by uncertainty about whether much public demand will arise for HDTV—quite aside from the particular transmission techniques it uses. No hard evidence exists to demonstrate that viewers are willing to pay much of a premium for higher-definition pictures on larger screens. Concerns are being increasingly expressed in broadcast circles about this point. As John Abel, Executive Vice President of the National Association of Broadcasters, asked, "Wouldn't it be a tragedy if we got [into digital broadcasting] and all we got out of it was better pictures—prettier pictures? We're not even sure consumers want prettier pictures."[43]

Rather than using digital channels immediately for HDTV, some parties see a greater potential for broadcaster use in multichannel NTSC video, interactive multimedia services, and other offerings in competition with cable and other multichannel providers. As expressed by Don West, editor of *Broadcasting and Cable*, "Left unchallenged, the FCC's insistence that digital be used exclusively for high definition will delay or deny to broadcasters a foothold in the digital generation. It will perpetuate the single channel as the standard for terrestrial television into the next century."[44] Press Broadcasting Company has proposed to the Commission "the immediate adoption of rules and standards permitting television broadcasters to utilize digital compression technology to provide, on the second 6 MHz channel already allotted

---

43. Sean Scully, *NAB Plays Multimedia Matchmaker*, BROADCASTING & CABLE, Apr. 19, 1993, at 44 (quoting John Abel).
44. BROADCASTING & CABLE, Aug. 17, 1992, at 12.

to them in connection with the Advanced Television (ATV) rule-making, multichannel program services."[45]

Similarly, Senator Conrad Burns, a member of the Senate Subcommittee on Communications, has recommended to Congress and the FCC that broadcasters be allowed to adopt digital compression and become multichannel program providers. "Policymakers should not expect broadcasters to continue to provide one video channel or audio channel while regulating the provision of that single 'broadcast only' channel under the 'public interest' standard . . . . Broadcasters' competitors are not similarly restrained."[46]

These concerns call current FCC policy into question. The Commission has engaged in advanced spectrum planning, even including the phaseout of analog broadcasting, based only on speculation and conjecture about what the public wants and is willing to pay for. It has grounded its plans on over-the-air transmission of HDTV even though a strong presumption exists that few HDTV viewers will be dependent on over-the-air transmission. Here, the comments of Commissioner Sherrie Marshall are telling:

> I am becoming increasingly convinced . . . that the real key to broadcasters' continued competitiveness lies not so much in ATV as a crisp picture, but in its potential for spectrum-efficient multiplexing. In my view, broadcasters must become multichannel providers to continue to flourish in the long run.[47]

If multichannel broadcasting does emerge, it will do so only after a painful redirection of FCC policy marked by prolonged and heated debate. Such troubling questions as the following will loom prominently:

   1. Should analog NTSC broadcasting be continued into the indefinite future (contrary to current FCC plans)?

---

45. Press Broadcasting Company, Inc., Petition for Rulemaking, at i (Aug. 24, 1992).
46. BROADCASTING & CABLE, June 29, 1992, at 56.
47. *Advanced Television Third Report and Order, supra* note 38, 7 F.C.C. Rec. at 6999-7000 (statement of Commissioner Sherrie P. Marshall).

2. If so, what minimum levels of conventional NTSC service should be maintained, which local broadcasters are to provide it, and can they rely on advertising for adequate financial support?

3. Would it be in the public interest to devote the current levels of spectrum allocated to analog broadcasting to a combination of analog broadcasting, multichannel NTSC service, and HDTV? If so, what mechanism should be used to determine who supplies what?

4. If digital transmission is to be used for multichannel NTSC broadcast, why not auction off the spectrum rights to the highest bidder, rather than giving the rights without payment to incumbent local broadcasters?

5. If incumbent local broadcasters are to be assured a long-term viable role, would it make sense, in terms of efficient spectrum use, to confine them to analog broadcasting plus expansion into multichannel NTSC service, while relying on other delivery mechanisms (for example, cable and DBS) for HDTV?

For our purposes, the most notable point is that years will be consumed in grappling with such questions. If local broadcasters do emerge as multichannel competitors to cable operators and other providers, they will do so only, when, out of the smoke and heat, a drastically refocused FCC policy toward spectrum use and local broadcasting is in place.

Conclusions

Despite the widespread interest in the use of fiber for video services by the LECs, competition with cable is more likely to come from wireless systems, at least during this decade. As with competitors in other fields, each system has its own strengths and weakness—characteristics that lead to competition among multichannel providers and wider consumer choice.

During the next few years, wireless cable will have an advantage in offering service at lower prices than cable or DBS operators, but with more limited channel capacity. That capacity will, nevertheless, be enough to carry programming with the greatest proven subscriber appeal.

Direct broadcast satellites will carry more channels, but with a substantial up-front equipment cost to subscribers. Handicapped by the inability to carry local television signals, DBS systems will be limited in subscribership to geographical areas with good over-the-air reception. Both wireless cable and DBS systems will offer excellent reception quality (to homes able to receive the signal) compared with present cable systems.

Cable systems will continue to have advantages in freedom from line-of-sight restrictions and outdoor antennas, while offering the full range of present and prospective services. Rates to subscribers, which will vary substantially among localities, will make cable more competitive with alternatives in some places than others.

In the longer run, LMDS may also be a strong contender. But questions of signal characteristics and system costs complicate our assessment at this early date.

Also in the longer run, the use of video compression may enable local broadcasting stations to transmit multichannel signals by using digital channels now planned for HDTV. Such use, however, raises troublesome issues about the FCC's plans for local broadcasters to provide HDTV, and eventually to end NTSC service. The spectrum capacity now planned for HDTV may well be more socially valuable for lower-resolution multichannel broadcasting or for quite different purposes, such as for mobile radio. But any shift in FCC policy can be expected only after years of review, heated debate, and legal challenges.

8

Overarching Policy Issues

EARLIER CHAPTERS HAVE ADDRESSED basic economic and technical comparisons between cable and alternative multichannel technologies, along with public policy issues pertaining directly to those comparisons. Here, we broaden our attention to issues that cut across technologies, and thus can best be addressed together. These issues fall under five categories: (1) the definition of effective competition; (2) local franchising, regulation, and public-service obligations; (3) the promotion of universal service; (4) cross-ownership between wireline and nonwireline networks; and (5) access to programming by competing video providers.

As before, our objective is to identify policies that will encourage the emergence and survival of those firms best able to meet the needs of consumers. In such an environment, firms with the lowest costs (for given outputs) are the ones most likely to flourish, rather than those that succeed because of either their anticompetitive activities or the handicaps imposed on their rivals through misguided regulatory and legislative constraints.

Defining Effective Competition

Recall the two key ingredients of effective competition as defined in the 1992 Cable Act: (1) the franchise area is to be served by one or more multichannel competitive alternatives to cable, each offering programming comparable to that of cable to at least 50 percent of the households, and (2) at least 15 percent of the households sign up with an alternative to cable. These criteria are troubling because competition, in any meaningful sense, cannot be identified solely by reference to a market-share test.[1] Vigorous competition is easily imaginable even if it fails the test. Conversely, the test could be satisfied with seriously constrained competition. This situation is especially worrisome because cable operators are to be subject to rate regulation until they face effective competition, as defined by the Act. Thus, the more successfully cable operators compete, the longer will be the time required for rivals to attain a 15 percent market share, and the longer will cable operators be regulated.

To explore the problem, let us turn to four questions: (1) When is effective competition, as defined by the Act, likely to be achieved? (2) Why is a better definition needed? (3) What will be the consequences for the cable industry of the FCC's use of the current definition? (4) What is a better way of determining whether effective competition exists under given circumstances?

Prospects for Effective Competition. The number of television households at year-end 1992 was about 93 million, of which 89 million, or 96 percent, were passed by cable.[2] Drawing from experience, we can estimate that about 96 million homes will be passed by cable by the end of the decade.[3] Thus, cable would generally be subject to effective competition at that time only if at least 14 million households had signed up for a multichannel service other than that of the incumbent cable system.

Attaining the 15 percent threshold will not be easy. By year-end 1993, probably no more than 4 million households were subscribers to

1. For a thorough analysis of this point, see William A. Landes & Richard A. Posner, *Market Power in Antitrust Cases*, 94 HARV. L. REV. 937 (1981). The contestability literature is also highly relevant. *See* WILLIAM J. BAUMOL, JOHN C. PANZAR & ROBERT D. WILLIG, CONTESTABLE MARKETS AND THE THEORY OF INDUSTRY STRUCTURE (Harcourt Brace Jovanovich, rev. ed. 1988).

2. NATIONAL CABLE TELEVISION ASS'N, CABLE TELEVISION DEVELOPMENTS 1-A (Mar. 1993).

3. During the ten-year period 1982–92, the number of television homes grew from 83.7 million to 93.1 million. PAUL KAGAN ASSOCS., CABLE TV INVESTOR, Feb. 12, 1993, at 5. If the same growth rate (in terms of average annual number of households added) continues during 1992-2002, 6.6 million homes will be added by year-end 1999. If the percentage of homes passed by cable remains constant at 96 percent, about 96 million homes will be passed by cable at the end of the decade.

TABLE 8–1
SUBSCRIBERS TO ALTERNATIVE
MULTICHANNEL SYSTEMS, YEAR-END 1999
(millions)

System	
Subscribers required for "effective" competition	14
Current subscribers (1993)	4
Satellite-based systems	5
Wireless cable, LMDS	3
Multichannel broadcasting	?
LEC wireline	?
Shortfall, year-end 1999	2

a multichannel competitor to cable (Table 8–1). This total consists of some 3 million HSD units in cable areas (of a total of about 4.4 million HSD units)[4] and perhaps another million from SMTVs, cable over-builds, wireless cable, and medium-power direct broadcast satellites. It would be surprising if as many as 10 million households were added to the 4 million by the end of the decade—all the more surprising since alternatives to cable will compete not only with cable, but also among themselves.

DBS is a leading potential competitor, in part because once a satellite is operational, most of the nation's households will have service "available" as stipulated in the 1992 Act. How quickly DBS, combined with other alternatives to cable, can reach the threshold of 15 percent sign-up will depend on the range of programming offered by DBS and the cost of home satellite receiving terminals. DBS will carry the sort of national programming that has a proven mass appeal, but the severe

4. In 1989, about 42 percent of the nation's HSD terminals were reported to be used by households in cable areas. This percentage has probably increased with the continual geographical expansion of cable. SATELLITE TV WEEK, Sept. 20, 1989.

limitations on carrying signals of local broadcasting stations is a drawback, especially in areas with poor over-the-air reception.

Even if DBS service meets with strong public enthusiasm, a sustained sign-up rate of more than a million households annually (including SMATV-based sales) is unlikely. Recall from Figure 6–1 that annual HSD sales reached no more than 750,000 units in the record year 1985. That total was attained when (1) HSD users received many more channels than were available over local cable systems and without payment for programming; (2) cable was more limited in geographical coverage than today; and (3) other multichannel alternatives, such as wireless cable, were not available. Under these circumstances, it is unrealistic to expect that DBS service will greatly exceed that record total on a sustained basis, even granted that future DBS systems will permit smaller and less-expensive satellite receivers. In Table 8–1, DBS is projected to have no more than 5 million subscribers by the year 2000.

Wireless cable, especially if adapted for use with video compression, also has good potential to compete with cable. Its major handicap is the shadow areas caused by low antenna angles and line-of-sight constraints associated with microwave transmission. Wireless cable might have as many as 3 million subscribers, perhaps about half that of DBS. Some DBS growth will come at the expense of wireless cable. Conversely, rapid growth of wireless cable would reduce the prospects for DBS. These two transmission systems are close substitutes, insofar as both would draw from viewers willing to install antennas in lieu of less obtrusive wireline connections.

Another contender, listed in Table 8–1, is multichannel transmission from local broadcasting stations. As discussed in Chapter 7, subscribership during this decade is highly uncertain because of the complex problems of spectrum management and regulatory policy that must be resolved before the service can be implemented. If service is eventually approved—and we cannot be certain that it will be—broadcasters will not be notable players in the multichannel market until the next century.

Another wireless system, LMDS in the 28 GHz band, is a possibility for this decade. But not enough is known about the technical and economic characteristics to venture a projection of subscribership. At best, its growth would largely be at the expense of wireless cable and DBS, with the use of 28 GHz providing substantial channel capacities even without signal compression.

Finally, what about wireline transmission, particularly in the hands of the LECs? As discussed in Chapter 3, satisfactory development of ADSL would encourage LEC entry into video by enabling the use of existing copper networks. As a useful, though speculative, illustration of the prospects for the LECs, consider the following: Suppose that ADSL does enjoy technical breakthroughs so that LECs can enter the video market by early 1995. Suppose further that an average sign-up rate of 1.5 million households annually is achieved—an annual growth about half of that recorded by the cable industry for its basic service sign-ups during the period 1975–92, when cable faced little multichannel competition.[5] According to this projection, the LECs would gain 7.5 million subscribers. Simply added to the levels in Table 8-1, this number would put the total over the threshold of 14 million subscribers. Because this growth would come partially at the expense of DBS and wireless cable, however, the total growth of subscribership to alternative multichannel systems would remain unclear.

If, in contrast, ADSL does not pan out, the LECs will be in greater difficulty. For the reasons discussed in Chapter 3, reliance on fiber and coaxial cable to bring video to the home is questionable in the face of vigorous competition from incumbent cable operators. Even if advanced wireline networks are sufficiently attractive to enable LEC entry into video, the process of building wholly new facilities will be time consuming.

A further complication arises. Even if the nationwide total of 14 million subscribers were achieved, cable systems would not be widely regarded as effectively competitive, as defined by the 1992 Cable Act. The growth of competitive alternatives to cable undoubtedly will be uneven across the nation. The 15 percent threshold may emerge in some geographical areas, thereby subjecting local cable systems to effective competition (and, hence, to rate deregulation), while shortfalls persist elsewhere. Perhaps a nationwide subscriber level of something

---

5. NATIONAL CABLE TELEVISION ASS'N, *supra* note 2, at 2-A. A growth rate for LEC video as high as 50 percent of that recorded by cable is optimistic, since cable operators would be expected to respond vigorously to such a competitive threat by the LECs.

like 16–17 million, rather than the 14 million in Table 8–1, would be needed before most geographical areas were subject to effective competition.

How can this cautious view of LEC entry be squared with the ambitious plans announced by Bell Atlantic, Pacific Bell, U S West, and others to wire millions of homes for broadband service by the year 2000? The point is simply thus: if near-term demands for new services (illustrated in Table 3–2) require such enormous channel capacities that new broadband networks, rather than cable upgrades, are needed, the LECs will contribute prominently to effective competition. Otherwise, we can expect delays, indefinite holds, and cancellations, while the LECs soberly reassess their prospects of competing with well entrenched cable operators.

Inappropriate Use of Market Share Data. In Chapter 5 the use of market share data was emphasized in measuring the degree of horizontal concentration. Focusing on the portion of the industry held by a single entity is important in evaluating the degree to which that entity can exert control. But market share data alone are not good measures of competitive pressures of concern here. The behavior of cable operators will be greatly affected by the *threat* of entry, quite aside from the actual subscribership recorded by competing networks. Especially with their nationwide coverage, DBS systems will be poised to exert competitive pressure only loosely tied to actual DBS subscriber sign-ups. High prices for cable service or poor performance in given local areas will encourage DBS entry, with possibly severe financial consequences for affected cable operators. The greater the degree of vigilance by cable operators over their rates, service offerings, and quality, the smaller the actual intrusion of DBS will be. At the same time, the impact of threatened DBS entry and its market growth will depend on its prices to subscribers and performance, which we cannot confidently predict.

The role played by the threat of entry is well illustrated by cable's response to the LECs. Surely, the rash of announcements about planned expansion of cable service through fiber and video compression, along with the development of new program services, is a direct response to the threat of LEC entry. Although this study concludes that the LECs will have great difficulty penetrating the video market (unless

ADSL proves out), many cable industry participants will disagree with that assessment—or, at least, they will not want to take any chances. Responding aggressively through bold new plans for network expansion will either forestall LEC entry or strengthen cable's position if the LECs do enter.

In short, cable will be under competitive pressure during the remainder of the 1990s, even if effective competition as defined by the Cable Act is not achieved. Thus, cable will continue to be subject to rate regulation.

A Regulatory Twilight Zone for Cable. The combination of rate regulation and competitive pressures will place the cable industry in much the same position that the telephone industry has faced ever since the FCC decided in 1959 (in the *Above 890* decision[6]) to permit large firms to use microwave facilities to meet their internal communications needs as an alternative to relying on the Bell System. Despite the increasing levels of competition since that time, AT&T in the interexchange field and the LECs in local services have remained subject to extensive government regulation. A persistent policy issue since the *Above 890* decision has revolved around the appropriate degree and timing of "streamlined" regulation or deregulation in response to growing competition. Among the difficulties, the degree of competition that has actually existed at any time has been the subject of controversy.

Similar problems will plague the cable industry. Cable operators seeking to respond to competition will be hobbled by regulation. Investment plans for upgraded networks in response to competition may involve additional costs that can be recovered only by raising subscriber rates for some services. But attempts to raise rates may trigger consumer complaints and prolonged deliberations by both local franchising authorities and the FCC. In the other direction, price cuts in some local areas, perhaps in response to threatened entry by wireless cable networks, may be met by complaints of predatory pricing, which will lead to costly and prolonged regulatory review. The cable industry will face difficult times in the regulatory arena, while new business

6. Allocation of Frequencies in the Bands Above 890 Mc, Dkt. No. 11866, 27 F.C.C. 359 (1959), *recon. denied*, 29 F.C.C. 825 (1960). See the discussion in MICHAEL K. KELLOGG, JOHN THORNE & PETER W. HUBER, FEDERAL TELECOMMUNICATIONS LAW 591-97 (Little, Brown & Co. 1992).

opportunities and new challenges continue to emerge in the highly dynamic telecommunications field.

Remedial Action. Congress erred in including in its legislation a definition of effective competition tied to a few simple criteria. The task of deciding whether effective competition exists within a given set of circumstances should have been left to the FCC. The Cable Act should be amended accordingly.

In discharging its tasks under an amended Cable Act, the Commission would need to weigh a number of factors, some not easy to handle. Among the questions are the following:

- Can competitors easily enter and exit the market? Large upfront investments may make entry difficult, especially if the assets, once committed, cannot be moved to other markets.

- Can newcomers easily increase their availability of service if the incumbent raises prices or reduces quality? An advantage of DBS systems with nationwide coverage is their widespread accessibility to consumers who might switch from the incumbent firm. This threat would reduce the incumbent firm's market power, even with a small DBS market share.

- Is the incumbent markedly reducing prices (in real terms) and offering new services? Such behavior may be in response to competitive pressure, even if rivals have not yet entered the market.

- Are the selling prices for the incumbent's assets falling relative to the replacement value of the assets? If so, the decline in the Tobin q ratio[7] toward, or equal to, unity would indicate an increasingly competitive market.

---

7. As evidence of the limited degree of competition in cable television, many have pointed to the high selling prices of existing cable systems (more than $2,000 per subscriber) relative to construction costs (in the neighborhood of $700 per subscriber). *See, e.g.,* Paul W. MacAvoy, *Tobin's* q *and the Cable Industry's Market Power,* MM Dkt. No. 89-600 (1990) (filed on behalf of the United States Telephone Ass'n). For a contrary view of the validity of measuring market power by dividing the market value of the firm by the replacement costs of its assets (the "Tobin q ratio"), see Sanford Grossman, *On the Misuse of Tobin's* q *to Measure Monopoly Power,* MM Dkt. No. 89-600 (1990) (filed on behalf of the National Cable Television Ass'n).

- Are the services of newcomers close substitutes for those of the incumbent? If, for example, the LECs were to offer only VCR-quality movies and other stored material on ADSL-equipped transmission facilities, the offerings would be primarily competitive with videocassette rentals and sales. Cable operators might retain market power in the broader video arena, even if the LECs attained a penetration above the 15 percent threshold.

Franchising, Regulation, and Public Service Obligations

Franchising requirements and public-service obligations imposed by local governments are a major impediment to fair and full competition among the technologies treated in this study. The burdens imposed on firms—depending on their choice of technology—will lead to capricious outcomes hardly in accord with the public interest.

With continuing technological advances and new opportunities, it will become increasing important to modify existing regimes for government intervention if all firms are to compete under the same ground rules. The problem is well illustrated by comparing the situations faced by cable operators and by LECs.

State Versus Local Jurisdiction. The legal basis for the local franchise requirements lies in the cable operator's need for access to public rights of way. To compensate for costs imposed on society, cable operators can properly be charged for the inconveniences imposed by trenching through streets and for other disruptions.

But franchise agreements go beyond compensation for these costs. Because cable has been widely regarded as a monopoly with the potential to earn large excess profits, municipalities have sought to extract for themselves some of this excess by imposing additional requirements on cable operators. Examples are levies on revenues, provision of institutional networks to serve government offices as well as other public users, and facilities for local program origination. During the bidding wars of the 1970s and early 1980s, cable operators agreed to heavy obligations in return for potentially lucrative franchises. In discharging these obligations, the cable industry faces some 13,000 local jurisdictions, with only six states exercising authority at the state level.[8]

---

8. National Ass'n of Regulatory Utility Commissioners, The Status of

The telephone industry, too, involves wireline networks with needs for public rights of way. Again, a valid reason exists for imposition of franchise requirements. But the franchise (and regulatory) authority for local service is generally defined at the state, not at the municipal, level. Telephone companies have certain obligations, most notably the provision of universal service and operation in accordance with common-carrier requirements. But they are not subjected to the burdens faced by cable operators. Telephone companies are not obliged, for example, to provide free telephone service to schools and government offices or to make financial contributions to civic activities. Rather than extracting a share of telephone monopoly profits for public use, state regulators have sought to reduce or eliminate monopoly profits by controlling intrastate telephone rates.

The differences in the regulatory regimes for the two industries pose two problems. First, difficulties arise for video competition between LECs and cable operators. Suppose that breakthroughs in ADSL technology permit rapid entry by the LECs into the video market. Suppose, further, that Congress eliminates the cross-ownership ban in accordance with the FCC's recommendation. Then the LEC would be free to engage in "cable television" as defined in the 1984 Cable Act. As the Commission recognized in its video dialtone order, however, the LEC would be required to obtain a local franchise.

Telephone companies already hold franchises generally granted at the state level. Would the need for two franchises unduly burden LECs in competing with cable operators? No general answer is possible because of the hodgepodge of arrangements resulting from historical accidents. To promote fair competition, the two entities should be subject to the same franchise burdens for their competing video activities.

The second problem arises with competition between the two entities in nonvideo markets. Entry by cable systems into nonvideo services raises the question whether these services should be assigned to state or to local jurisdictions. The answer depends on answers to other questions:

1. If states are to exercise jurisdiction, how are costs to be sepa-
    rated between the nonvideo services that fall under state juris-
    diction and the video services that fall under local jurisdiction?
    Would procedures to separate costs and outcomes create con-
    flict between the jurisdictions and add to the risks and the
    delays faced by cable ventures?

2. If local governments are to exercise jurisdiction, would cable
    operators, dealing with some 13,000 jurisdictions for their
    nonvideo services, be at a disadvantage in competing with other
    nonvideo providers (including the LECs) that deal at the state
    level?

3. If local governments are to exercise jurisdiction, do they have
    the staff and expertise to oversee nonvideo services, especially
    when concerns have already been widely voiced that they lack
    the resources to regulate even *video* services as directed by the
    1992 Cable Act?

At the same time, the argument has been advanced that regulatory
authority should, with exceptions, be left to the jurisdiction that most
closely fits the relevant market.[9] If, for example, the relevant market
for cable television is local video distribution, it should be regulated at
the local level, not at the state or the federal level.

In this regard, cable is becoming less local as a consequence of
continuing technological opportunities. The Pennsylvania Cable Television Association, for example, has established a program—the
FiberSpan project—to tie together cable systems throughout the state
with fiber and microwave radio links.[10] This effort is aimed at encouraging the development of new broadband and narrowband services
by spreading programming costs over a larger subscriber base enabled
by statewide coverage. The Michigan Cable Television Association is
moving in the same direction with an engineering study and comprehensive data collection needed for construction of a statewide intercon-

9. *See* Timothy J. Brennan, *Local Government Action and Antitrust Policy: An Economic Analysis*, 12 FORDHAM URB. L.J. 405, 428–29 (1984).
10. PENNSYLVANIA CABLE TELEVISION ASS'N, FIBERSPAN PENNSYLVANIA (1993).

nected network. Florida, Georgia, Illinois, New Jersey, and Tennessee are considering similar actions.[11] With such developments, it is increasingly difficult to say that cable service is any more local than is local telephony. Indeed, if statewide cable coverage becomes a reality while the LECs continue to be prohibited from entering the interLATA market, the reverse will increasingly be true.

All in all, it seems easy to conclude that the local franchising and regulatory process should be abolished, with all such functions moved to the state level. The advantages of state over local oversight are perhaps best brought home by posing the simple question: How many readers advocate that the oversight function for *local telephone companies* be transferred from the states to the municipalities?

Public-Service Obligations. Problems with the current structure for oversight arise with other competitors to cable. DBS and other wireless technologies not requiring access to public rights of way are free of franchising requirements. Is this situation fair? Although not requiring public rights of way, wireless systems use scarce radio spectrum space that they get for "free." In return for radio spectrum, should not public-service obligations be imposed on wireless systems? Congress answered in the affirmative by stipulating in the 1992 Cable Act that the FCC determine what public-service obligations should be imposed on DBS. Accordingly, the Commission issued a notice of proposed rulemaking to determine the appropriate set of obligations:

> Section 25 of the 1992 Cable Act, which added new section 335 to the Communications Act of 1934, as amended, requires the Commission to impose on providers of direct broadcast satellite service video programming obligations which must include, at a minimum, the political programming requirements set forth in sections 312(a)(7) and 315 of the Communications Act of 1934. In addition, section 25 requires the Commission to adopt rules governing the reservation and availability of channels for noncommercial educational and information programming at reasonable rates. Finally, the Commission must examine the opportunities that

---

11. WARREN'S CABLE REGULATION MONITOR, Nov. 8, 1993, at 1-2.

the establishment of DBS service provides for fulfilling the Commission's longstanding goal of service to local communities.[12]

The requirements imposed on DBS by the 1992 Act are troubling. The FCC will face a daunting task in seeking to impose public-service obligations on DBS comparable to the franchise and public-service obligations of cable operators. For DBS systems, with their national or regional coverage, it is infeasible to impose local community-access requirements equivalent to those faced by cable operators. An alternative might be a regional or national DBS access requirement. But would such access contribute much to society in light of the deluge of nationally oriented channels already available on multichannel systems? The objective must not be to impose obligations on DBS just because such burdens are imposed elsewhere. If obligations are to be imposed at all, they should be crafted to provide value to society.

Moreover, if DBS is to be burdened, what about wireless cable, which also uses spectrum for free? Local public-access requirements would be more feasible for wireless cable, but another complication arises. These systems obtain much of their capacity from part-time use of channels licensed to community colleges and other educational users. Alongside their own program offerings, many wireless operators are carrying these educational channels into classrooms and other places that otherwise would not be served. Thus, wireless operators are already performing a useful social function. It is questionable whether additional public-service obligations should be imposed, especially in light of the severe channel-capacity constraints within which wireless cable must work.

As a substitute for public-service obligations, one might advocate an annual fee on all wireless systems in return for their use of scarce radio spectrum. But why should DBS and wireless cable systems be singled out for such payments when other spectrum users—common-carrier microwave, mobile radio, and such—continue their use of spectrum for free?

---

12. Implementation of Section 25 of the Cable Television Consumer Protection and Competition Act of 1992, Direct Broadcast Satellite Public Service Obligations, Notice of Proposed Rulemaking, MM Dkt. No. 93-25, 8 F.C.C. Rcd. 1589, 1589 ¶ 1 (1993).

The fundamental problem lies in the *quid pro quo* approach to today's assignments of spectrum rights. In exchange for spectrum rights without direct payment, certain users must perform public-service functions. The difficulty with this approach is twofold. First, regulators have little basis for determining the social value of the public-service obligations that they impose. It is easy to imagine circumstances in which these obligations confer little social value, while inflicting substantial costs on the providers.

Second, regulators have no way to value the spectrum rights that they assign. The value of these rights could be quite high or essentially zero, depending on the demands by potential alternative users for the spectrum rights in question. Only by sheer coincidence would the value of the spectrum rights be equal to the value of the public services performed in exchange.

Consequently, it is time to recognize squarely the inefficiencies of the current system of assigning spectrum rights. Whether determined through the use of lotteries or public hearings, spectrum users have gained rights to a valuable public resource without payment. A critical breakthrough in national policy was achieved in the Omnibus Budget Reconciliation Act of 1993, which authorizes the Commission to award license for spectrum use through a competitive bidding process.[13] In response, the Commission has proposed that auctions be limited to "(a) mutually exclusive applications, (b) initial license applications (and not renewal or modification applications), and (c) radio communications services that principally use their spectrum to provide service to subscribers for compensation."[14] Thus, radio and broadcasting licenses would not be included.[15] The Commission has tentatively concluded that competitive bidding begin with PCS services along with a few other services, including "certain cellular radio service applications."[16]

---

13. Pub. L. No. 103-66, 107 Stat. 312, 387-96 (1993) (codified at 47 U.S.C. § 309(j)).
14. Implementation of Section 309(j) of the Communications Act, Competitive Bidding, Notice of Proposed Rule Making, PP Dkt. No. 93-253, 8 F.C.C. Rcd. 7635, 7635 ¶ 2 (1993).
15. *Id.*
16. *Id.* at 7635 ¶ 3.

This auctioning authority is a landmark step toward assigning spectrum rights to their most socially valuable uses. It also provides a basis for a policy *to reduce* or *to eliminate* public-service obligations, rather than devising new obligations (as for DBS). Substitutes for these obligations would consist of (1) a franchise requirement on wireline operators limited to the costs imposed on society caused by disruption of public rights of way and (2) payments for radio spectrum use by DBS and other users of radio spectrum, through use of auctions, to reflect the market value of this scarce resource.

This approach raises three questions. First, if the burden on wireline franchises is limited only to the cost of accessing public rights of way, what about the public-service obligations, fees based on revenues, and other burdens that cable operators now face? These burdens have nothing to do with public rights of way. Rather, they are imposed by franchisers to share in the monopoly profits that cable operators are presumed to earn from holding the franchises. In an increasingly competitive market, any ability to earn excess profits will disappear. As this franchising strategy becomes increasingly outmoded, municipalities will face increasing pressures to relax the burdens imposed by franchises. This process will mark the appropriate time to move the franchising and regulatory jurisdiction to the state level.

Second, the use of auctions for new spectrum assignments may be feasible enough for new wireless systems, but what about incumbent users? In response to political pressures, implementation of auctions may be accompanied by the grandfathering of existing users. In this event, the best course of public action may simply be to accept the fact that these users will have some advantage over their competitors as a consequence of incumbency. Attempts by the FCC to promote fairness by imposing special fees on incumbent spectrum users will probably fail, while imposition of special public-service obligations on newcomers will probably be ill advised. In the best of attainable worlds, the playing field will still have some bumps.

Third, will it be feasible to limit franchising only to systems that require public rights of way, as assumed above? According to a Supreme Court decision involving SMATV systems, the need for public rights of way is not the only rationale for the requirement to obtain a local franchise.[17] The Court distinguished between SMATV systems that connect buildings that belong to a single owner or are commonly managed, and those that connect buildings belonging to separate owners or are separately managed. Neither system required public rights of way. In the first case, "all the subscribers could negotiate [with the SMATV operator] through the common owner or manager,"[18] thereby protecting their interests. Thus, regulatory safeguards conferred by the local franchise would not be essential for subscribers in commonly owned or managed complexes. With separately owned complexes, in contrast, one SMATV operator could gain a foothold by signing up one complex and installing a satellite dish on one of the buildings. From there the SMATV operator

> would enjoy a powerful cost advantage in competing for the remaining subscribers: he could connect additional buildings for the cost of a few feet of cable, whereas any competitor would have to recover the cost of his own satellite headend facility. Thus, the first operator could charge rates well above his cost and still undercut the competition. This potential for effective monopoly power might theoretically justify regulating the latter class of SMATV systems and not the former.[19]

The possibility also exists that the SMATV operator, free of franchising requirements, may *more* effectively compete with the local cable operator for subscribers. The Court, however, did not consider this alternative way of protecting subscriber interests.

We need not debate here whether the Court's opinion has merit. But whatever regulation is to be imposed on SMATV operators or on other telecommunications providers, jurisdiction should reside at the state rather than at the local level.

17. FCC *v.* Beach Communications, Inc., 113 S. Ct. 2096 (1993).
18. *Id.* at 2103.
19. *Id.*

Universal-Service Obligations

Similar to long-standing concerns about maintaining universal telephone service in the face of competition, issues arise about whether, and how, universal service should be assured for multichannel video offerings. To illustrate, suppose a cable operator provides universal geographical coverage in its franchise area as required under the franchise agreement. Suppose further that the local LEC proposes also to supply video service. Should the LEC be required also to provide universal coverage?

In the near term at least, the LEC should *not* be required to offer universal video coverage. Moreover, the cable operator should be *relieved* of its obligation to provide universal coverage and be given, at the same time, pricing flexibility in response to competition from the LEC and other multichannel rivals.

This perhaps surprising response is consistent with the results of the preceding discussion. There we emphasized the need to reduce or eliminate cable's public-service obligations as mandated by the franchise, because these obligations—like the obligation to provide universal coverage—will become increasingly inappropriate as competitive pressures mount.

To support these conclusions, we note first the two dimensions of universal service: (1) widespread geographical coverage of the network to permit access to anyone willing to pay for service and (2) service "affordable" enough to enable most households to hook into the universally available network. To illustrate these two dimensions of access and affordability—and the troubling issues that they present for policy makers—we consider two hypothetical scenarios. The first emphasizes differences in network cost, the second differences in competitive pressures, within the cable franchise area. In both, we assume that the economics of LEC competition with incumbent cable operators are more favorable than is depicted in Chapter 3.

Scenario 1: Differences in Network Cost. The Acme Cable Company serves the Windward franchise area, consisting of two subareas: densely populated High Density and sparsely populated Low Density. The entire area is flat, with good over-the-air reception from a half-dozen television broadcasting stations. As a requirement in the franchise,

166 Toward Competition in Cable Television

written in 1980, Acme has covered the entire area with a coaxial cable system carrying thirty channels. Because construction and operating costs are high in Low Density, however, Acme is not able to cover its incremental costs there from Low Density revenues. It agreed to provide service to Low Density only because revenues from High Density, where costs are much lower, are sufficient to cover the shortfall, and because its agreement was necessary to win the franchise in competition with other cable bidders. The LEC in Windward supplies universal telephone service, whose preservation is not an issue here.

By the mid-1990s, Acme faces competition quite unforeseen during the late 1970s, when it was vying for the Windward franchise. Both DBS and wireless cable services become available in the entire area, while the LEC proposes to build a broadband network in High Density. It does not plan to extend the network into Low Density, however, because of long distances between customer locations.

Acme is in a tight situation. It plans to upgrade its network to be competitive with the LEC's proposal in High Density. With potentially declining revenues in High Density, however, combined with the cost of the network upgrade, it can no longer afford to subsidize service in Low Density. It will continue with the existing network in Low Density but plans to abandon service to Low Density when the network needs replacement. Hence, households in Low Density would not have access to either the LEC or the Acme advanced network.

This scenario raises a number of questions:

• Should the LEC be required to extend its proposed advanced network to serve Low Density? To require it to do so would be difficult because, facing competition from Acme and from wireless operators, the LEC also would be hard pressed to subsidize service in Low Density.

• Should Acme be required to extend its proposed upgrade to include Low Density? Doing so may be met by Acme's ultimatum that either it serves only High Density with the advanced network, or it pulls out of Windward entirely, leaving the LEC with a monopoly of wireline service.

- Does service from DBS and other wireless systems count toward universal coverage? We have implicitly assumed that universal coverage is measured in terms of wireline service. Yet, wireless systems easily cover Low Density. To be sure, the offerings differ somewhat from those on an advanced wireline system (for example, satellites do not carry locally broadcast signals), and the presence of buildings, trees, and other obstructions in Low Density would deny wireless access to some homes.

- Would the answers to the preceding questions differ if it were known that the overwhelming bulk of viewing in Low Density will be of mass entertainment programming, regardless of which networks are available?

Fundamental here are the differences between video and telephone service. The widely held view that universal telephone service is important enough to deserve subsidy in some cases is based on the notion either that the value of the network to one individual increases as the number of others connected to the network expands, or that telephone service plays such a vital role in safety and welfare as to justify subsidies for households unable to pay.

In contrast, why should we care whether our neighbors subscribe to cable television, even if it offers 500 channels? We should care if at least one of these conditions exists: (1) interactive services among individuals are widely developed, beyond those possible on telephone networks, with the value of the video network to one individual depending on how many others are connected, and (2) the network provides such valuable educational or other socially meritorious functions that it deserves subsidy for the same reasons that society supports, for example, formal education.

We are far from seeing such interactive services becoming commercially viable. In the near term, the wise course is to permit the players wide latitude to market *whatever services they wish, wherever they wish.* To burden them with universal-coverage obligations (or other public-service obligations) would threaten to foreclose business ventures that might otherwise confer impressive societal benefits.

All this leaves open the obvious question. Suppose there does emerge a panoply of broadband interactive, interpersonal services or ones so vital to safety or welfare that, as with today's telephone service, universal broadband coverage becomes a legitimate policy goal. How would that goal best be achieved? This question leads to complex issues about who should pay subsidies, who should receive them, and how, in particular cases, the magnitude of the appropriate subsidy should be assessed.

One possibility is a pooling of contributions from competitors to support service in high-cost areas, similar to proposals commonly made for preserving universal telephone coverage.[20] This approach, however, could lead into dangerous territory. Were wireless systems taxed and the proceeds used to benefit their wireline competitor in its high-cost area also served by the wireless systems, competition from these wireless sources might be weakened. This situation is different, say, from a levy paid by a CAP to support the LEC's operations in high-cost areas because the CAP (unlike wireless operators) would compete with the LEC only in low-cost areas, not in high-cost ones. Indeed, it is the CAP's reluctance to enter high-cost areas that would justify a contribution to support universal service supplied by the LEC. The CAP's contribution, while a burden on it, would not at the same time be used to strengthen the LEC in a market in which the CAP competes—unlike the case of wireless systems.

We leave to others a detailed analysis of the issues here. They will plague policy makers for years to come—if services developed on video networks do, in fact, attain such social significance that access to them deserves subsidy.

Scenario 2: Differences in Competitive Pressures. Consider a franchise area called Leeward that is exactly the same as Windward except that Low Density is hilly instead of flat. This topographical difference forecloses competition by wireless systems in Low Density because of line-of-sight constraints, while also degrading reception from local broadcasting stations. Because Low Density is more attractive for cable than in Scenario 1, Acme would have been willing to cover all of

---

20. *See, e.g.*, Proposal to the Commission for a "Universal Service Assurance Fund" *in* Petition of MFS Communications Company, Inc. for a Notice of Inquiry and En Banc Hearing (Nov. 1, 1993).

Leeward with its thirty-channel coaxial system, even without a franchise agreement about universal-service obligations.

As before, competition emerges in the mid-1990s. DBS and wireless cable systems attract subscribers in High Density's flatland. The LEC again proposes to build an advanced network in High Density. Because Low Density is more attractive for wireline service than in Scenario 1, the LEC leaves open the possibility of extending the network to Low Density, where revenues may be enough to offset the large outlays involved.

In response, Acme proposes to upgrade its network in High Density to remain competitive with the LEC's capability. But it is troubled about advanced services to Low Density. Competition in High Density from wireless systems is forcing it to reduce rates there. Moreover, under section 623(d) of the 1992 Cable Act, which mandates a uniform rate structure throughout the franchise area, Acme must also reduce rates in Low Density to match those in High Density.[21] At such low rates, Acme cannot cover the cost of an advanced system in Low Density. The LEC is in the same predicament. No uniform price within the franchise area would enable either one or both together to cover the cost of advanced systems in Low Density. Consequently, under the constraint of rate uniformity, neither proceeds to build in Low Density.

At the same time, Low Density residents, with their degraded reception from broadcasting stations and little access to multichannel wireless services, are quite willing to pay higher rates to obtain the advanced services available in High Density. The obvious solution is a *higher* rate structure in Low Density than in High Density. Fully understanding this and many similar situations, Congress is moved to repeal section 623(d), which mandates uniform rate structures. In response, both Acme and the LEC proceed to build advanced networks in Low Density, with residents benefiting from two-wire competition.

But we aren't out of the woods yet. Subscribers in Low Density complain about the high rates. "Vital broadband services are being denied to low-income families," some exclaim, "because rates are unaffordable." Others point to the disparities between "information haves" and "information have nots." Yet others cannot understand why

21. 47 U.S.C. § 543 (d).

they should pay more than their friends in High Density for the same services, and from the same companies.

The solution to the affordability problem is easier than remedies for the network coverage problem in Scenario 1. Here, we can draw directly from telephone experience. After dealing for decades with questions of affordability, policy makers generally agree that targeted subsidies to those who otherwise could not afford telephone service are superior to broad subsidies under which, for example, rates to all residential subscribers are kept low at the expense of long distance-users. Accordingly, for qualifying households, most states have adopted lifeline programs involving discounted monthly service rates and Link-Up America programs involving discounts on service connection charges.[22] Such approaches would be suitable for broadband services—provided that they evolve in ways that merit subsidy.

Cross-Ownership Between Wireline and Wireless Systems

Going beyond the telephone company–cable television debate, under what conditions should cross-ownership be allowed across alternative technologies used in common service territories? More specifically, under what conditions would cross-ownership likely confer public benefits—or be anticompetitive? How does current and prospective FCC policy stand in light of this answer?

Cable and Wireless Cable. To increase the competitive potential between cable and wireless cable, the FCC decided in 1990 to impose a general ban on cross-ownership between cable and wireless cable within common service territories.[23] The 1992 Cable Act codified the ban and extended it to SMATV systems.[24] In response, the Commis-

---

22. For an assessment of the early history of these programs, see LELAND L. JOHNSON, TELEPHONE ASSISTANCE PROGRAMS FOR LOW-INCOME HOUSEHOLDS (RAND 1988). Updated status reports are periodically issued by the Industry Analysis Division of the Commission's Common Carrier Bureau.

23. Amendment of Parts 21, 43, 74, 78, and 94 of the Commission's Rules Governing Use of the Frequencies in the 2.1 and 2.5 GHz Bands Affecting: Private Operational-Fixed Microwave Service, Multipoint Distribution Service, Multichannel Multipoint Distribution Service, Instructional Television Fixed Service, and Cable Television Relay Service, Report and Order, Gen. Dkt. Nos. 90-54, 80-113, 5 F.C.C. Rcd. 6410, 6417 ¶ 42 (1990).

24. Pub. L. No. 102-385, 106 Stat. 1460, § 11(a) (amending 47 U.S.C. §533 (a)).

sion amended its rules in mid-1993.[25] No ban now exists, however, between cable and DBS systems; a number of cable operators hold ownership shares in Primestar, as discussed earlier.

Potential benefits from the existing ban on common ownership of cable and wireless cable clearly seem to exceed potential losses. Few, if any, economies of scope exist between the two in transmission. Coaxial cable, fiber, trenches, conduits, and line amplifiers have little in common with microwave transmitting towers and residential microwave receiving equipment.

One area of potential synergy between the two is in marketing, customer relations, and administration. Given the similarity of the end product—many channels of television—cost savings might accrue if a single entity performed these functions within each local community. But these savings, if they exist at all, are surely small relative to the potential benefits of competition between the two systems.

The situation with SMATV systems is less clear-cut insofar as a synergy does exist with cable. The internal wiring of apartment buildings and other high-density housing complexes has much in common with other residential wireline systems. Even so, the competitive gains from the cross-ownership ban may outweigh the transmission economies of scope. Operators of high-density housing developments would have greater freedom of choice between being served by the local cable system or by the competing SMATV systems, if the networks are independently owned. Without a cross-ownership ban, an important component of the potential SMATV customer base could be lost.

Direct Broadcast Satellites and Cable. What about DBS, for which no cross-ownership ban with cable exists? The situation is much the same as with wireless cable. Network design and operation exhibit weak or nonexistent economies of scope. For the same reasons as with wireless cable, a cross-ownership ban seems justified.

There is a twist here, however, by virtue of the regional or national coverage afforded DBS—in contrast to wireless cable—that lessens the threat of anticompetitive behavior. Anticompetitive use of DBS by

25. Implementation of Sections 11 and 13 of the Cable Television Consumer Protection and Competition Act of 1992, Horizontal and Vertical Ownership Limits, Cross-Ownership Limitations and Anti-Trafficking Provisions, Report and Order and Further Notice of Proposed Rule Making, MM Dkt. No. 92-264, 8 F.C.C. Rcd. 6828 (1993).

cable operators would presumably take the form of deliberately reducing the attractiveness of DBS service as a competitive alternative to their existing and potential cable subscribers. But this failure to exploit the full potential of DBS would benefit *all* cable operators within the service area of the DBS system. Thus, cable operators that pursue such an anticompetitive strategy would suffer all the losses of not taking full advantage of DBS technology, while the benefits of the strategy would be largely conferred on other cable operators—free riders here—that are sheltered from competition from DBS.

The distribution of these losses and gains depends on the cable market shares within the DBS service area held by the cable operators with ownership shares in the DBS system. A combination of large MSOs collectively holding 100 percent ownership of a DBS venture would be worrisome insofar as these operators *would* stand to capture the bulk of the benefits from limiting the development of DBS. Conversely, the same combination that holds collectively only a small share, say, 5 percent, of the satellite venture would pose little threat since the other (noncable) owners would presumably resist any strategy that would artificially restrict the attractiveness of their DBS venture.

An additional constraint on anticompetitive behavior is the possibility of entry by other, independently owned DBS systems, which would be encouraged if the cable-owned DBS venture were not permitted to compete freely with cable systems.[26] The numerous orbital slots assigned for high-power DBS increases the potential for such competitive entry.

The gains from a cross-ownership ban in terms of foreclosing anticompetitive behavior would probably not be large, but the losses from a ban, in terms of lost economics of scope, seem even smaller. On balance, society may have more to gain than to lose from a cross-ownership ban on cable and DBS systems, as a structural safeguard to complement antitrust enforcement, discussed in Chapter 5.

---

26. One could argue that such limitations on wireless cable by its cable owners would also encourage entry by competing wireless systems. But here problems of spectrum constraints intrude. Spectrum availability for a single wireless system is severely limited (a current maximum of thirty-three channels). Splitting this number among two or more competing applicants would be problematic. In contrast, the eight orbital slots (each with a capacity of thirty-two uncompressed channels) set aside for DBS afford wide opportunity for competition among DBS systems.

Access to Programming

The history of multichannel competition with cable has been marked by concerns that competitors have been denied access to programming under reasonable terms. As noted in an FCC report, wireless cable operators have paid 36–70 percent more per subscriber for six cable network services than cable operators have.[27] SMATV systems have paid a per-subscriber premium of $2.25 and $2.64 per month for HBO and Showtime, respectively, over the rates reportedly paid by one cable MSO.[28] Complaints have focused on vertical ties with programmers; cable operators were alleged to have denied programming to their competitors, or to have made it available only on discriminatory terms.

In response to such disparities, section 628(b) of the 1992 Cable Act provides:

> It shall be unlawful for a cable operator, a satellite cable programming vendor in which a cable operator has an attributable interest, or a satellite broadcast programming vendor to engage in unfair methods of competition or unfair or deceptive acts or practices, the purpose or effect of which is to hinder significantly or to prevent any multichannel video programming distributor from providing satellite cable programming or satellite broadcast programming to subscribers or consumers.[29]

Section 628(c) instructs the Commission to adopt regulations to specify the particular conduct prohibited by such stipulations. The Commission's regulations are to (1) establish safeguards to prevent undue influence by cable operators upon actions by affiliated program vendors related to the sale of programming to unaffiliated distributors; (2) prohibit price discrimination by vertically integrated satellite cable programming vendors and satellite broadcast programming vendors; and (3) prohibit exclusive contracts between a cable operator and a

---

27. Competition, Rate Deregulation, and the Commission's Policies Relating to the Provision of Cable Television Service, Report, MM Dkt. No. 89-600, 5 F.C.C. Rcd. 4962, 5117 tbl. XI (1990) [hereinafter *1990 Cable Report*].

28. *Id.* at 5118 tbl. XII.

29. 47 U.S.C. § 548(b).

vertically integrated programming vendor in areas that are not served by a cable operator and any such exclusive arrangements in areas served by cable that are not found in the public interest by the Commission.[30]

In April 1993, the Commission issued rules that offer broad protection for competitors to cable systems. Especially important are the lowered evidentiary burdens for programming-access complainants. Where vertical integration is an essential element of a complaint, "the complainant need show only that the relevant programmer or cable operator is vertically integrated in any market."[31] Furthermore, the Commission has adopted a strict attribution standard for assessing the presence of vertical integration: all equity interests of 5 percent or more are included.[32]

Program exclusivity arrangements are severely restricted. Exclusive arrangements between vertically integrated programmers and operators in areas not served by a cable operator are "illegal *per se* and may not be justified under any circumstances."[33] Moreover, exclusive contracts in areas served by cable (except those entered into before June 1, 1990) may not be enforced unless the Commission first determines that the contract serves the public interest.[34]

In addition to these congressional and FCC actions, antitrust suits brought by forty state attornies general and by the Department of Justice have led to consent decrees with the cable MSOs that are partners in the Primestar DBS system. According to the DOJ complaint,

The MSO defendants, through their control of access to over 50 percent of the nation's cable subscribers, can limit the incentives of nondefendant cable programmers to deal with competing DBS ventures by their ability to threaten or actually take retaliatory actions, such as refusing to promote the programmer's program-

30. *Id.* § 548(c)(2). *See also* Implementation of Sections 12 and 19 of the Cable Television Consumer Protection and Competition Act of 1992, Development of Competition and Diversity in Video Programming Distribution and Carriage, First Report and Order, MM Dkt. No. 92-265, 8 F.C.C. Rcd. 3359, 3361 ¶ 3 (1993).
31. *Id.* at 3363 ¶ 11.
32. *Id.*
33. *Id.* at 3364 ¶ 16.
34. *Id.*

ming within their franchise areas, assigning an unfavorable service tier or channel position to the programming, charging a high price for the programming if it is a premium service, and, sometimes, refusing to carry the programming at all.[35]

Under the settlement, programming controlled by these companies—HBO, Cinemax, MTV, Showtime, The Movie Channel, and others—is to be made available to DBS and other noncable services at nondiscriminatory prices.[36]

A notable characteristic of such nondiscrimination requirements is that they may be hard to enforce because of the complexity of program-use agreements and differences in costs and risks that are hard to quantify. Price differences for programming acquisition may reflect a number of considerations rather than constituting evidence of anticompetitive conduct. With SMATV and wireless cable, for example, the Disney Channel has stated that per-subscriber wholesale rates are higher than cable operator wholesale rates "to account for higher administrative and marketing costs, bad debts, and problems with signal security."[37] ESPN has not licensed programming to some wireless cable operators "because of problems relating to signal theft, financial stability and distribution capabilities."[38] It is easy to imagine that disputes about discriminatory treatment, involving questions of costs, risks, and other factors, will constitute a rich source of future litigation.

Mandated nondiscriminatory access to programming can best be regarded as a backup safeguard to the limitations on horizontal concentration discussed in Chapter 5. If a cable operator controls a particular program network but has only a tiny share of the national market of cable subscribers, the operator would have no incentive to discriminate against noncable systems in selling program rights to them. Discrimi-

---

35. Plaintiff's Complaint at ¶ 50, United States *v.* Primestar Partners, L.P., No. 93-3913 (S.D.N.Y. filed June 6, 1993).

36. United States *v.* Primestar Partners, L.P., Proposed Final Judgment and Competitive Impact Statement, 58 Fed. Reg. 33,944 (1993). *See also* United States *v.* Primestar Partners, L.P., Public Comments and Response on Proposed Final Judgment, 58 Fed. Reg. 60,672 (1993).

37. *1990 Cable Report, supra* note 27, at 5026 n.179.

38. *Id.*

nation would inflict a financial loss on the operator while other cable operators would be the primary beneficiaries of harm done to non-cable competitors. This is the same kind of free-rider problem earlier discussed with respect to DBS systems. It is only in cases where the cable operator has a substantial market share of subscribers or is in collusion with other cable operators that discrimination against outsiders would be a rational strategy.

Requirements for nondiscrimination in program sales is one of four basic ways to forestall anticompetitive behavior in program markets. The others are limitations on horizontal concentration and channel-occupancy limits (Chapter 5) and nondiscriminatory network access to programmers (a key ingredient of video dialtone in Chapter 4). As discussed, video dialtone may be nonviable because, applied only to the LECs, it handicaps them in competing against incumbent cable operators, who are free of such obligations. Channel-occupancy limits, under some circumstances, may not prevent anticompetitive behavior. Nondiscrimination in program sales will be hard to enforce. Limitations on horizontal concentration are potentially the most effective of these by directly reducing or eliminating the incentives of the cable operator to engage in anticompetitive behavior.

Conclusions

In this chapter, we have reached six primary conclusions. First, in writing the 1992 Cable Act, Congress erred in defining effective competition with cable in terms of a simple market-share criterion, rather than leaving judgments about competition to the Commission. Although the prospects for competition with cable are good, the chances are remote for achieving by the end of the decade widespread effective competition as defined in the 1992 Cable Act. It is unlikely that combined subscribership of DBS, wireless cable, and other multichannel alternatives to cable will reach the minimum level stipulated by the Act as a condition for effective competition. Nevertheless, even if that level of subscribership is not attained, cable will face a good deal of competitive pressure. This situation will be difficult for cable operators because, even though facing competition, their rates will be subject to regulation under terms stipulated in the 1992 Act until effective competition as defined in the Act is achieved.

Second, an impediment to even-handed competition, likely to worsen with integrated offering of telephone and video, is the split between state and local jurisdictions. As a consequence of historical accident, states have jurisdiction over local telephone service while, generally, local jurisdictions exercise oversight over cable. All such functions should be consolidated in the hands of the states.

Third, the imposition of public-service obligations on carriers in exchange for a cable franchise or other valuable privileges is increasingly inappropriate as competition becomes more pervasive. Ideally, wireline operators should be limited in their obligations only to compensate for the disruptions along streets and other public rights of way resulting from the installation of their facilities. Wireless operators should be forced to pay for their rights to use spectrum as a reflection of the opportunity cost of spectrum use, best measured in the auction marketplace. Continuation of today's policies will result in the use of some technologies being burdened, and others not, in arbitrary and capricious ways.

Fourth, obligations by cable operators and others to provide universal network coverage will become increasingly inappropriate as competition grows. The parallel obligation to offer service affordable to low-income groups, if broadband service evolves to serve vital social needs, can best be met by targeted subsidies similar to those already in place for telephone service.

Fifth, the Commission should consider extending the cross-ownership ban between cable and wireless cable to include more generally a prohibition of ties between wireline and wireless systems. The stimulus to competition from doing so is likely to more than offset any forgone economies from joint ownership and operation.

Sixth, the provisions for nondiscriminatory access to programming by rival multichannel providers can best be regarded as a complement to limitations on horizontal concentration. If these limitations prove inadequate, the nondiscriminatory access provisions, though difficult to enforce, may help to assure access to programming under reasonable terms.

9

A Note of Optimism

THINK BACK TO 1980. Since then, cable systems have become accessible to more than 95 percent of the nation's homes; cable program networks fed by satellite links have multiplied by the dozens; a plethora of on-line information services has emerged for businesses, libraries, schools, and, increasingly, homes; more local broadcasting stations have come onto the air; the videocassette market has passed the $12 billion per year mark; interactive home entertainment on video cartridges has shown strong appeal; and we are witnessing rapid development of CD-ROM applications with a far richer assortment of interactive offerings. Applications of computer technology have been nothing short of staggering, with skyrocketing sales of personal computers, followed by laptops and notebooks.

Developments to the end of the century and beyond will be no less exciting. Video channels will multiply into the hundreds, new services will continue to blossom, and consumers will enjoy lower-cost access to an ever-growing menu of entertainment, educational, and business offerings.

Fortunately, these developments do not critically depend on the widespread deployment of any one technology or on the success of particular firms. The possibilities are so numerous, in terms of alternative technologies and the roles of diverse firms, that the public will benefit almost regardless of which path is taken through the maze. The challenge for public policy is to facilitate and to guide this dynamic process in ways that maximize these benefits.

This study has focused on two aspects: (1) the directions from which competition in the cable television market is likely to arise in light of technical, economic, and public policy constraints, and (2) identification of ingredients in a legislative and regulatory framework geared to ensuring that whichever firms survive the competitive struggle will be those best able to meet evolving consumer needs.

Winners and Losers

Despite the widespread interest that has been expressed in the potential of fiber for video services provided by the LECs, they will have an uphill struggle in competition with incumbent cable operators. The primary reasons are that (1) cable operators already pass more than 95 percent of the nation's homes with broadband facilities, (2) they can more easily upgrade their networks than the LECs can for expanded broadband services, and (3) they can as easily exploit the economies of scope in combining video and telephone services on the same network.

The prospects for the LECs to compete in the video market with cable operators would be improved, at least during this decade, if they could use their existing copper networks for satisfactory video transmission, rather than investing tens of billions of dollars in new networks. Alternatively, if the demand for new interactive services required such enormous increases in channel capacity that new networks rather than upgrades of existing facilities were needed, the LECs would be in a stronger position to overcome the first-mover advantage enjoyed by cable operators.

For three reasons, we must be cautious about the prospects for mushrooming new service markets in response to construction of advanced networks. First, many of the commonly mentioned new services could be supplied with combinations of today's telephone and cable networks. The stumbling block is not the absence of fiber but insufficient consumer demand to offset the high cost of software development. Second, we have yet to see resounding successes from the numerous experiments and field trials in recent years. Third, many new services will be partial substitutes for each other and for existing services. A strong demand for one will be, in part at least, at the expense of others.

Alliances between telephone companies and cable MSOs will be procompetitive insofar as (1) incumbent cable operators, able to draw from telephone company expertise, will be better able to enter telephone markets and (2) the LECs, similarly drawing from cable company expertise, will be better positioned to enter their in-territory video markets. They will face formidable competition, however, from incumbent cable operators who themselves will be strengthened by ties with the telephone industry. Whatever substantial competition emerges between the LECs and cable operators in this decade is at least as likely to arise in telephone as in video markets.

Of key importance in promoting competition is adequate protection against undue horizontal concentration in the video marketplace. Moreover, the cable MSO must divest itself of any cable holdings within the operating territory of any telephone company with which it has ownership ties.

Beyond wireline rivalry, direct broadcast satellites have strong potential for competing with cable. With nationwide or regionwide satellite coverage, tens of millions of households have an alternative for receiving dozens of television channels. Even if only a small percentage of households subscribe to DBS systems, cable operators will face pressure to maintain low rates and high service standards—as expected in a competitive industry.

The success of DBS systems will hinge on the cost of home satellite receivers and on consumer reaction to the range of services offered. Widespread geographical coverage renders infeasible on-demand video service and carriage of signals from numerous local broadcasting stations. At the same time, DBS operators may take the lead in offering HDTV.

By substituting less costly microwave transmission for wireline networks, wireless cable systems are another promising competitor for cable. The main handicaps are limited channel capacity, because of spectrum limitations, and line-of-sight transmission constraints that render service to some households difficult or impossible. Success will depend largely on the ability of wireless operators to multiply capacity with digital compression technologies, while undercutting the prices of comparable cable offerings.

In the longer run, the use of video compression may enable local broadcasting stations to transmit multichannel signals with digital channels now planned for HDTV. Such use, however, raises troublesome issues about the FCC's plans for local broadcasters to provide HDTV and eventually to end NTSC service. The FCC's emphasis on transmission of HDTV signals by terrestrial broadcasting seems misdirected because most viewers willing to buy expensive HDTV receivers will probably subscribe to a multichannel wireline or wireless service, rather than depending on over-the-air broadcast. If so, HDTV broadcasters will serve essentially as HDTV programmers to cable and other multichannel providers, while transmitting signals over the air to a small or virtually nonexistent over-the-air audience. The spectrum space now planned for HDTV may well be more valuable for multichannel lower-resolution broadcasting or for quite different applications, such as mobile radio. But any shift in FCC policy can be expected only after years of heated debate, review, and legal challenges.

National Goals: A Cautionary Note

We must beware of one pitfall in moving ahead: establishment of "national goals" defined in terms of specific outcomes to be achieved. A leading example is the talk nowadays about the need for an "information superhighway" and the consequent requirement to frame legislative and regulatory policies to achieve that goal. No one has come up with an acceptable working definition of the superhighway. Worse, the phrase conveys the notion that there should be but *one* information conduit, as if packaging together all telecommunications services were obviously the most desirable of all outcomes. In fact, we have many information highways—some at the cutting edge of technology, some in need of repair, and some needing to be junked. Surely, many more highways will be built. Some will diverge while others converge. Together, these can be thought of as a superhighway. Better to avoid such catchphrases, which only obfuscate terms of the debate, and to get on with the task of devising sensible public policies for guiding the telecommunications sector into the next century.[1]

1. As one wag put it, "what the telecommunications community needs is a new set of

If obfuscation were the only consequence, it would hardly be worthwhile to dwell here on such pitfalls. Some potential consequences, however, are more worrisome. Specifically, much talk has centered around achieving the "two-wire" outcome as a national goal.[2] In this case, the LECs and cable operators would find themselves in a sustained competitive relationship, with two video wires to every home. To be sure, we might hope that economic and technological factors evolve to permit such vigorous wireline competition. But enshrining that outcome as a national goal would be dangerous. To help ensure that outcome, legislators and regulators would be tempted to tilt the playing field. It is all too easy to imagine the pursuit of competition for competition's sake, divorced from sound economic and technical considerations.

Far better is the delineation of national policy in terms of sound *process*. Set the goal of establishing a regulatory and legislative framework that, relying on marketplace pressures, encourages firms to search out and to develop innovative ways to cut costs, to improve existing services, and to invent new ones. Thus, the process would be geared to ensuring not that particular technologies or services flourish, but rather that surviving firms are those best able to meet consumer needs. If viable two-wire competition emerges, fine. If, however, the outcome is one wire as a consequence of a wireline monopoly being demonstrated in the marketplace as the most efficient way to provide service, then live with the outcome and devise the best ways to protect against monopoly abuse. Throughout, two questions are paramount: How well is the process working? How can it be improved?

A Legislative and Regulatory Framework

With the goal of seeking ways to improve that process, this study suggests a number of tasks for Congress, for the FCC, and for state and local governments.

---

clichés."

2. Kim McAvoy, *Markey's Goal: Two Wires in Every House*, BROADCASTING & CABLE, Nov. 15, 1993, at 26.

Congressional Initiatives. Six items stand out for congressional action. First, legislation should be enacted to lift the court-imposed ban on interLATA carriage of video signals by the BOCs. This initiative is listed first, not because the interLATA restriction is the most important of all public policies that merit reappraisal, but simply because it is the one that, among all of them, makes the least sense.

Second, franchising and intrastate regulatory functions should be taken out of the hands of local jurisdictions and shifted to the states. The exercise by municipalities of these functions is an anachronism that poses an impediment to even-handed competition among the players.

Third, Congress should repeal section 623(d) of the 1992 Cable Act, which requires the cable operator to maintain a uniform rate structure throughout the franchise area. Cable operators should have the freedom to adjust rate structures in response to varying competitive pressures within franchise areas.

Fourth, Congress should revise the 1992 Cable Act to give the Commission the responsibility for determining conditions under which effective video competition exists. The existence of effective competition can be judged only by weighing a number of factors. Congress erred in defining effective competition in terms of a 15 percent market-share test. Under that test, the more vigorously cable operators compete against their rivals, the longer it will be before these rivals attain a 15 percent market share, and the longer will cable operators be rate-regulated. Although the prospects for competition with cable are good, at least from wireless sources, the chances are remote for achieving, by the end of the decade, widespread effective competition as defined in the 1992 Cable Act.

Fifth, Congress should recognize that the threat of cross-subsidy is essentially irrelevant to the debate about whether the cross-ownership ban should be lifted. The possibility of cross-subsidy arises not from telephone company ownership of programming or from control of content but from the shared use of transmission facilities by video and telephone signals. If the threat of cross-subsidy is deemed so great that the ban should be retained, Congress should move also to reverse the FCC's decision to permit LEC entry even into video dialtone, which presumably would be offered on networks shared by telephone and video services. Otherwise, Congress should lift the ban and permit the LECs to compete on full parity with cable operators.

With full parity, the LECs would have the same freedom to participate in program ownership and to discriminate among program suppliers as cable operators do today. Thus, LECs would not be singled out for common-carrier responsibilities, unlike the case under the FCC's video dialtone rules.

Perhaps surprisingly, the failure to meet the common-carrier objectives of greater information diversity, espoused by the Commission, may prove of little consequence to society. Common-carrier obligations would not necessarily expand the diversity of programming. With or without common carriage, diversity will expand with the growth in channel capacity and through competition with other multichannel providers such as wireless cable and DBS systems. Moreover, diversity will be favorably affected by telephone company involvement since the financial resources of the companies will encourage the production of programming that otherwise would not exist.

Aside from cross-subsidization, what about the threat of anticompetitive use of LEC network bottlenecks in the program market? This problem is no different for the LECs than for cable operators. If the threat is judged so serious that the cross-ownership ban should be retained, Congress would be obliged to consider seriously banning cable operators as well from holding ownership interests in programming. For both the LECs and cable operators, the appropriate safeguard against anticompetitive use of bottlenecks is a limitation on horizontal concentration.

Finally, if the LECs are permitted to compete on full parity with cable operators in the video market, parity should be assured also in the telephone market. A number of states have already opened their intraLATA toll and local exchange markets to competition. To accelerate the process elsewhere, legislation may be required to preempt state authority in order to implement a policy of open entry into intrastate telephone markets.

The Commission's Role. First, and most important, the Commission should reassess the adequacy of its safeguards against cross-subsidization by the LECs and make every effort to seek remedial action where necessary. Possibilities of cross-subsidization, emphasized throughout this monograph, pose the single most pressing—and difficult—problem facing policy makers in the LEC/cable television arena.

Second, the Commission should revisit its horizontal concentration rules. The 30 percent limit that it selected as the percentage of homes passed by a single cable operator may be too high. The greater audience fragmentation caused by continued increases in channel capacity may dictate that, to be financially viable, some programmers must have wider access to cable networks than the Commission considered during its deliberations.

Moreover, alliances between telephone and cable television suggest that telephone companies will play a larger role in out-of-territory cable operations than was appreciated at the time of the Commission's decision. This study concludes that this greater presence of telephone companies will be procompetitive rather than anticompetitive—but only if horizontal concentration is limited. The Commission should reconsider its decision in light of these factors.

Third, the Commission should consider extending its cross-ownership ban that now exists between a cable system and wireless cable or SMATV systems operating in its territory to include DBS systems, since DBS is potentially a prime candidate for competition with cable. Such structural safeguards may be a powerful complement to effective antitrust enforcement.

Fourth, the Commission should hesitate to impose public-service obligations on DBS systems or other multichannel providers. Such obligations are generally justified as an exchange for use of spectrum space without charge or for the right to a valuable local franchise. The better course is (1) to use auctions for assigning spectrum rights, (2) to encourage competition to reduce the value of franchises, and (3) to reduce or eliminate public-service obligations, since they would no longer be in exchange for special privileges.

Fifth, the Commission should review its policies toward the development of HDTV. Rather than transmitting HDTV, broadcasters may play a more important role as multichannel providers of video to low-income households and others unwilling or unable to pay for more expensive cable, DBS, or terrestrial wireless services.

The Role of State and Local Governments. First, the states should adopt policies of open access to local telephone exchanges, placing cable operators and other providers on a regulatory parity with the LECs in telephone service.

Second, franchising and regulatory responsibilities for cable systems should be shifted from local jurisdictions to state jurisdiction, in parallel with today's regulation of intrastate telephone service.

Third, state and local authorities should reduce or eliminate public-service and universal-coverage obligations on cable operators and others. Such obligations will become increasingly inappropriate as competitive pressures mount. If broadband services are shown eventually to merit subsidy, special assistance programs to ensure universal service can be established at that time—although not without facing a number of troublesome and complex issues.

Fourth, the states should continue to adopt and to perfect price-cap and other incentive programs for the regulation of intrastate telephone rates as a substitute for traditional rate-of-return regulation. Such approaches reduce (although they do not eliminate) incentives for subsidizing video ventures out of the pockets of telephone subscribers.

Strength Through Diversity

Any investigation of competition and public policy in such a dynamic arena is handicapped by uncertainties about future technological advances and social needs. The only certainty is that surprises are in store. Before the end of the decade, we must anticipate achievements and disappointments going far beyond anything foreseeable in this monograph.

In this environment of uncertainty, combined with widely perceived opportunities, we would expect a great diversity of initiatives, some succeeding, others failing, in line with marketplace pressures. Consequently, we should take heart in the array of hardware and software developments, experiments and field tests, business alliances and spin-offs, and, more generally, a high entrepreneurial willingness to take risk. The account of some new or innovative activity, reported almost daily it seems, bodes well.

To encourage and to direct these energies in ways that best serve the public interest, flexible policies must be framed to permit marketplace forces to work at best advantage. Here, too, the prospects are bright.

Needed actions by federal and state legislators, as well as the role of regulatory agencies, are reasonably clear cut. Although difficult problems remain and solutions will never be perfect, the American public will be the big winner.

Glossary

Analog transmission: Transmission of information by a continuous signal that fluctuates in frequency. In contrast to digital transmission.

Asymmetrical digital subscriber line (ADSL): Technology that allows multiple, simultaneous high-speed services to be carried over existing twisted pairs, thus dramatically increasing the potential of installed copper networks. Most of the capacity is devoted to distribution of video downstream to consumers.

Bandwidth: A measure of the information-carrying capacity of a channel. The more bandwidth a channel has, the more information it can carry.

Bell operating companies (BOCs): The twenty-two operating companies divested from the Bell System under the MFJ. They provide intraexchange transport of calls and local access to interexchange service.

Bell System: A term synonymous with the predivestiture American Telephone and Telegraph Company, which principally consisted of twenty-three local-exchange operating companies, Western Electric Company, Bell Laboratories, and Long Lines. Long Lines became the core of postdivestiture AT&T.

Bit: A binary unit of information that can have either of two values, 0 or 1. Contraction of binary digit. Kilobit = 1,000 bits; megabit = 1 million bits; gigabit = 1 billion bits; terabit = 1 trillion bits.

Broadband: Transmission speeds of 45 Mbps (45,000,000 bits per second) or greater. A single broadband facility of 45 Mbps can carry 672 voice conversations. Some broadband facilities have transmission speeds in the billions of bits per second (gigabits per second or Gbps).

Broadcast satellite service (BSS): Radio frequencies and orbital positions designated by the Federal Communications Commission for satellite television broadcasting directly to viewers.

Cellular telephony: A wireless telecommunications system, used extensively for mobile communications, that divides a geographic region into cells, uses a low-power transmitter within each cell, and reuses transmission frequencies in cells that are not contiguous.

Communications Satellite Corp. (COMSAT): A private organization created pursuant to the Communications Act of 1964 to serve as the U.S. signatory to INTELSAT.

Contiguous United States (CONUS): The forty-eight states within a single land mass; excludes Alaska and Hawaii.

Digital compression: A technique that enables a given message, such as a television picture, to be converted from an analog signal to a digitized code of data that occupies a smaller amount of transmission capacity than the original analog signal. This technique can effectively increase the amount of usable spectrum currently allocated and expand the number of available telecommunications channels.

Digital transmission: Transmission of information by converting it into binary form, that is, a series of 0s and 1s. In contrast to analog transmission.

Downlink: The transmission of radio signals from a satellite to an earth station.

Earth station: A ground station that use a a parabolic antenna (dish) to transmit to, or receive radio signals from, a satellite.

Fiber-optic network: A network made of glass or plastic cables that employs pulses of light to transmit large quantities of information.

Fixed satellite service (FSS): Radio frequency bands and orbital slots designated by the Federal Communications Commission for satellite communications to fixed locations on earth. In contrast to mobile locations (for example, ships at sea).

Geosynchronous orbit: A satellite orbit in which the satellite is deployed 22,300 miles above the equator. In this position, the speed of the satellite is synchronized with the speed of the earth's rotation so that the satellite appears stationary from any point on the earth's surface.

Instructional television fixed service (ITFS): A system of distributing television signals to schools and other qualified institutions by transmitting over the air in the 2 GHz radio frequency region.

Interconnection: The linkage of one telecommunications network to another, such as the linkage of an interexchange carrier to a local exchange carrier in order to complete a long-distance call.

Interexchange carrier (IXC): A telecommunications carrier, such as AT&T or MCI, that is authorized to provide "long-distance" service between local access and transport areas.

Ku-Band: The 11.7–12.7 GHz (gigahertz) frequency band. This band has been split into two segments by the FCC. The first is the 11.7–12.2 GHz band known as FSS (fixed satellite service). The 12.2–12.7 GHz segment is known as BSS (broadcast satellite service).

Lifeline service: A program designed to promote universal telephone availability by subsidizing basic service to qualifying households. Similarly, the Link Up America program subsidizes installation costs for qualifying households.

Local access and transport area (LATA): Following the AT&T divestiture, a local market for exchange services provided by a Bell operating company; pursuant to the Modification of Final Judgment, Bell operating companies may not transport calls across LATA boundaries but rather must switch them to interexchange carriers.

Local multichannel distribution service (LMDS): A system of distributing television signals over the air at relatively high radio frequencies (28 GHz) within cells a few miles in radius. In contrast to wireless cable, which uses lower frequencies (2 GHz) to broadcast over a radius of 30 miles or so.

Modification of Final Judgment (MFJ): The consent decree that effected the divestiture of AT&T and imposed various line-of-business restrictions on the regional Bell operating companies.

Multiple system operator (MSO): A cable television operator, such as Time Warner Inc. or Tele-Communications, Inc. (TCI), that provides service through more than one regional cable television system.

Narrowband: Transmission speeds of less than 64 kbps.

National Television System Committee (NTSC): A committee of industry representatives that agreed to the NTSC standard for black-and-white broadcast television in 1940 and for color television in the early 1950s.

Personal communications services (PCS): Any one of many prospective services or systems, such as pocket telephones, that provide direct wireless access by means of low-power cells analogous to those used in cellular telephony. Also called personal communications networks (PCN).

Rain fade: Radio signal interference caused by precipitation.

Regional Bell operating company (RBOC): One of seven regional companies that assumed ownership, following the AT&T divestiture, of the local exchange activities of the former Bell System. They are Ameritech, Bell Atlantic, BellSouth, NYNEX, Pacific Telesis, Southwestern Bell, and U S West.

Satellite dish: A parabolic antenna that collects satellite signals.

Satellite master antenna television (SMATV): Delivery of television by means of a satellite receiving antenna connected by wire to individual subscribers within close proximity to each other, usually within one or more apartment buildings.

Satellite receiver: A device capable of receiving and tuning satellite signals.

Server: A computer designed to receive, organize, and retrieve information quickly. It contains a storage system (usually a computer hard disc), high-speed input and output connections, and a program that keeps track of information in the system.

Television household: A group of individuals occupying a dwelling having one or more television sets.

Television receive only (TVRO): A satellite television receiving antenna and associated equipment.

Transponder: The component of a satellite that (1) receives an uplink signal, (2) shifts the frequency and amplifies the signal, and (3) retransmits it to the receiving earth station.

Trunk: A communications connection that is jointly used by a large number of customers.

Two-way cable system: A cable television system with the capacity to transmit signals to the headend as well as away from it. Two-way or bidirectional systems carry data and full audio and video television signals in either direction.

Ultrahigh frequency (UHF): The range of frequencies extending from 300 to 3,000 MHz; also, television channels 14 through 83.

Uplink: Transmission of a signal from a station on earth to a satellite for beaming back to a receiving earth station.

Very high frequency (VHF): The range of frequencies from 30 to 300 MHz. Includes television channels 2 to 13 and the FM band.

Wireless cable: See local multichannel distribution service.

References

Baldwin, T., and D. McVoy, *Cable Communication* (Prentice-Hall 1988).

Baran, Paul, "The Universal Communications System of the Future: Telephone or TV Cable?" (NCTA Cable Convention, San Francisco, June 8, 1993).

Baumol, William J., Michael F. Koehn, and Robert D. Willig, "How Arbitrary Is Arbitrary?—or, Toward the Deserved Demise of Full Cost Allocation," *Public Utility Fortnightly*, vol. 120, no. 5 (September 3, 1987).

Baumol, William J., John C. Panzar, and Robert D. Willig, *Contestable Markets and the Theory of Industry Structure* (Harcourt Brace Jovanovich rev. ed. 1988).

Baumol, William J., and David F. Bradford, "Optimal Departures from Marginal Cost Pricing," 60 *American Economic Review* 265 (1970).

Baumol, William J., and J. Gregory Sidak, *Toward Competition in Local Telephony* (MIT Press and AEI Press 1993).

Bell Atlantic, "Bell Atlantic, TCI and Liberty Media to Merge," News Release (October 13, 1993).

Bell Atlantic, "Bell Atlantic Accelerates Network Deployment," News Release (December 1, 1993).

Besen, Stanley M., and Leland L. Johnson, *An Economic Analysis of Mandatory Leased Channel Access for Cable Television* (RAND 1982).

Bilotti, Richard, Jr., Drew Hanson, and Richard J. MacDonald, *The Cable Television Industry: New Technologies, New Opportunities and New Competition*, vol. 1 (Grantchester Securities & Wasserstein Perella Securities March 8, 1993).

Braeutigam, Ronald R., and John C. Panzar, "Effects of the Change from Rate-of-Return to Price-Cap Regulation," 83 *American Economic Review Papers and Proceedings* 191 (1993).

Braeutigam, Ronald R., and John C. Panzar, "Diversification Incentives Under Price-based and Cost-based Regulation," 20 *RAND Journal of Economics* 373 (1989).

Brennan, Timothy J., "Local Government Action and Antitrust Policy: An Economic Analysis," 12 *Fordham Urban Law Journal* 405 (1984).

Brown, Rich, "Thomson Homes in on DBS Marketing," *Broadcasting and Cable*, December 20, 1993, at 59.

Bruce, Bob, "The Lure of Fiber Optics," *Public Power*, September-October 1993, at 16.

Cabinet Committee on Communications, *Cable: Report to the President* (G.P.O. 1974).

California Public Utilities Commission, *Enhancing California's Competitive Strength, A Strategy for Telecommunications Infrastructure* (November 1993).

CellularVision of New York, "CellularVision of New York in Partnership with Bell Atlantic to Roll-out Alternative Cable Services in New York," News Release (August 4, 1993).

Committee for Economic Development, *Broadcasting and Cable Television* (1975).

Communications Satellite Corporation, *1985 Form 10K* (1986).

Davis, Bob, "FCC to Grant Owner of Every TV Station Another License Free," *Wall Street Journal*, March 19, 1992, at 1.

Dawson, Fred, "Telco Video," *CableVision*, September 9, 1991, at 32.

Demsetz, Harold, "Why Regulate Utilities," 11 *Journal of Law and Economics* 55 (1968).

Donaldson, Lufkin & Jenrette, *Competition Is Emerging in the U.S. Telephone Market* (June 7, 1991).

Dukes, Ann, "Telesat Set to Overbuild Televents in FL," *Multichannel News*, March 14, 1988, at 36.

Dukes, Stephen D., *Next Generation Cable Network Architecture* (Cable Television Laboratories, Technical Papers, April 23, 1992).

FiberVision Corporation, "New Cable TV Company Offers Competing Service," News Release (July 8, 1993).

FiberVision Corporation, "New Company Cracks Cable TV Monopolies in Four Connecticut Franchise Areas," News Release (October 21, 1993).

Fink, Donald G., ed., *Television Standards and Practice: Selected Papers of the National Television System Committee and its Panels* (McGraw Hill 1943).

Fink, Donald G., ed., *Color Television Standards: Selected Papers and Records* (McGraw Hill 1955).

Fleming, E. Stephen, and Michael B. McLaughlin, "ADSL: The On-Ramp to the Information Highway," *Telephony*, July 12, 1993, at 20.

Flint, Joe, "Clash of the Titans, Fifth-Network Style," *Broadcasting and Cable*, December 20, 1993, at 38.

General Accounting Office, *1991 Survey of Cable Television Rates and Services* (July 1991).

Gilder, George, "Into the Fibersphere," *Forbes ASAP*, December 7, 1992, at 111.

Gilder, George, "Telecosm: The New Rule of Wireless," *Forbes ASAP*, March 29, 1993, at 96.

Glasgow Electric Plant Board, *Glasgow's Fully Interactive Communications and Control System* (1993).

Grand Alliance, "Digital HDTV Grand Alliance Makes Key Technology Decisions," News Release (October 21, 1993).

Grossman, Sanford J., "On the Misuse of Tobin's q to Measure Monopoly Power," filed in FCC MM Docket No. 89-600 on behalf of the National Cable Television Association, February 26, 1990.

Haddad, Charles, "Cable Industry under Air Attack," *Atlantic Journal*, November 26, 1993, at G4.

Haring, John, R., and Kathleen B. Levitz, "The Law and Economics of Federalism in Telecommunications," 41 *Federal Communications Law Journal* 261 (1989).

Hatfield Associates, *New Local Exchange Technology: Preserving the Bottleneck or Providing Competitive Alternatives?* (April 6, 1992).

Hawes, Karen J. P., "Encryption in the '90s," *Via Satellite,* June 1990, at 29.

Hazlett, Thomas W., "Duopolistic Competition in Cable Television: Implications for Public Policy," 7 *Yale Journal of Regulation* 65 (1990).

Howard, H. Taylor, "C-Band Antennas in a 2 Degree Spacing Environment," *1991 World Satellite Annual* at 4-1 (Mark Long Enterprises 1991).

Huber, Peter W., Michael K. Kellogg, and John Thorne, *The Geodesic Network II, 1993 Report on Competition in the Telephone Industry* (Geodesic Company 1992).

Hughes Communications, "USSB Signs with Hughes for High-Power DBS Satellite Transponders," News Release (June 3, 1991).

Hughes Communications, "Hughes Selects Thomson and News Datacom to Provide DirecTV Receiving System," News Release (February 3, 1992).

Illinois Commerce Commission, *Local Competition and Interconnection*, Staff Report, July 1, 1992.

Jessell, Harry A., "Video Dialtone Falls Short for Telcos," *Broadcasting*, February 10, 1992, at 48.

Johnson, Leland L., *Telephone Assistance Programs for Low-Income Households* (RAND 1988).

Johnson, Leland L., *Common Carrier Video Delivery by Telephone Companies* (RAND 1992).

Johnson, Leland L., Affidavit, Exhibit E, New Jersey Cable Television Association, Reply to Opposition to Petition of the New Jersey Cable Television Association to Deny, W-P-C 6840 (February 17, 1993).

Johnson, Leland L., and Deborah R. Castleman, *Direct Broadcast Satellites: A Competitive Alternative to Cable Television?* (RAND 1991).

Johnson, Leland L., and David P. Reed, *Residential Broadband Services by Telephone Companies* (RAND 1990).

Kellogg, Michael K., John Thorne, and Peter W. Huber, *Federal Telecommunications Law* (Little, Brown & Co. 1992).

Keyworth II, George A., and Bruce Abell, *Competitiveness and Telecommunications* (Hudson Institute 1990).

Klein, Benjamin, "The Competitive Consequences of Vertical Integration in the Cable Industry" (University of California, Los Angeles, Working Paper, June 1989), Attachment to National Cable Television Association, Comments, MM Docket No. 92-264, February 9, 1993.

Landes, William A., and Richard A. Posner, "Market Power in Antitrust Cases," 94 *Harvard Law Review* 937 (1981).

Lippman, John, "Tuning Out the TV of Tomorrow," *Los Angeles Times*, August 31, 1993, at 1.

Local-DBS Inc., Comments, MM Docket No. 93-25 (May 21, 1993).

Loral Corporation, "Space Systems/Loral Receives $400 Million to Contract for Two Direct-to-Home Broadcast Satellites," News Release (July 26, 1993).

McAvoy, Kim, "Markey's Goal: Two Wires in Every House," *Broadcasting and Cable*, November 15, 1993, at 26.

MacAvoy, Paul W., "Tobin's q and the Cable Industry's Market Power," filed in FCC MM Docket No. 89-600 on behalf of the United States Telephone Association, February 28, 1990.

Markey, Edward J., Statement before United States Telephone Association, October 4, 1993, at 6.

Manchester, Earl E., "New Uses for Residential Copper," *Telephony*, June 10, 1991, at 34.

MFS Communications Company Inc., Petition for a Notice of Inquiry and En Banc Hearing (November 1, 1993).

Moshavi, Sharon D., "Time Warner Unveils 150 Channels," *Broadcasting*, December 23, 1991, at 18.

"Municipally Owned Cable Television Systems," 51 *Public Power* 156 (January-February 1993).

Narrod, Debbie, "Overbuilders Get Serious," *Cable World*, March 5, 1990, at 22.

National Association of Regulatory Utility Commissioners, *NARUC Report on the Status of Competition in Intrastate Telecommunications* (November 9, 1993).

National Cable Television Association, "Facts Concerning the Status of the Home Satellite Dish Industry and Scrambled Programming" (November 1989).

National Cable Television Association, Comments, MM Docket No. 92-266, January 27, 1993.

National Cable Television Association, *Cable Television Developments* (March 1993).

Nordberg Capital, Inc., *Third Generation Television* (October 21, 1993).

Owen, Bruce M., Affidavit (May 20, 1993) and Affidavit (June 9, 1993), Chesapeake & Potomac Tel. Co. of Va. v United States, No. 92-CV-1751-A (E.D. Va. filed Dec. 17, 1992).

Pacific Bell, "Pacific Bell Invests in California's Communications Superhighway," News Release (November 11, 1993).

Paul Kagan Associates, "Cable TV Overbuild Census," *Cable TV Franchising Data Roundup*, April 30, 1992.

Pacific Telesis Group, *1992 Form 10-K* (1993).

Pennsylvania Cable Television Association, "FiberSpan Pennsylvania," (1993).

Pepper, Robert M., "Through the Looking Glass: Integrated Broadband Networks, Regulatory Policies and Institutional Change," 4 *Federal Communications Commission Record* 1306 (1988).

Performance Systems International, Inc., "PSI and Continental Cablevision Announce Plans to Deliver Internet over Cable TV," News Release (August 1993).

Posner, Richard A., "The Appropriate Scope of Regulation in the CATV Industry," 3 *Bell Journal of Economics* 98 (1972).

President's Task Force on Communications Policy, *Final Report*, (GPO, 1968).

Press Broadcasting Company, Inc., Petition for Rulemaking, August 24, 1992.

Reed, David P., *Residential Fiber Optic Networks, An Engineering and Economic Analysis* (Artech House 1992).

Reed, David P., *Putting It All Together: The Cost Structure of Personal Communications Services* (FCC Office of Plans and Policy, Working Paper Series No. 28, November 1992).

Reed, David P., "The Prospects for Competition in the Subscriber Loop: The Fiber to the Neighborhood Approach" (Twenty-first Annual Telecommunications Policy Research Policy Conference, September 1993).

Rubinovitz, Robert, "Market Power and Price Increases for Basic Cable Service since Deregulation," 24 *RAND Journal of Economics* 1 (1993).

Satellite Broadcasting and Communications Association, *Satellite TV* (undated).

Satellite Broadcasting and Communications Association, Comments, National Telecommunications and Information Docket No. 920532-2132, 1992.

Scully, Sean, "NAB Plays Multimedia Matchmaker," *Broadcasting and Cable*, April 19, 1993, at 44.

Scully, Sean, "Primestar Buys Compression for $250M," *Broadcasting and Cable*, August 9, 1993, at 49.

Setzer, Florence, and Jonathan Levy, *Broadcast Television in a Multichannel Marketplace* (FCC Office of Plans and Policy, Working Paper Series No. 26, 1991).

Shepherd, William G., "Contestability vs. Competition," 73 *American Economic Review* 572 (1984).

Sikes, Alfred C., "The Future of Interactive Communications" (Annual Business Week Symposium on Information Highways, New York, September 11, 1991).

Smiley, Albert K., "Regulation and Competition in Cable Television," 7 *Yale Journal on Regulation* 121 (1990).

Sloan Commission on Cable Communications, *On the Cable* (McGraw-Hill 1971).

Southwestern Bell Corporation, "Southwestern Bell Corporation, Cox Cable Communications Sign Agreement to Form U.S. Cable Television Partnership," News Release (December 7, 1993).

Tanner, Craig K., *Digital Compression and Transmission* (Cable Television Laboratories November 1992).

"Telesat Sells Out to Palmer in Two Florida Counties," *Multichannel News*, August 14, 1989, at 22.

Time Warner, Inc., "Time Warner Entertainment and U S West Close Strategic Parntership Investment," News Release (September 15, 1993).

UHF Comparability Task Force, FCC Office of Plans and Policy, September 1980.

U.S. Congress, House Committee on Energy and Commerce, Cable Television Consumer Protection and Competition Act of 1992, House Report 628, 103d Cong., 1st Sess. (June 29, 1992).

U.S. Congress, Senate Committee on Commerce, Science, and Transportation, Cable Television Consumer Protection Act of 1991, Senate Report No. 92, 102d Cong., 1st Sess. (1991).

U S West, "U S West Communications to Build Mass-Market Video Network," News Release (February 4, 1993).

Wall, G., R. Poirier, and A. Boucher, *The DBS Report* (Canadian Cable Television Association, 1992).

Waterman, David H., and Andrew A. Weiss, "The Effects of Vertical Integration between Cable Television Systems and Pay Cable Networks" (Annenberg School for Communication and Department of Economics, Univ. of Southern Calif., Working Paper, March 1993).

Waterman, David H., and Andrew A. Weiss, "Vertical Integration in Cable Television" (American Enterprise Institute Working Paper, Sept. 17, 1993).

Williamson, Oliver E., "Franchise Bidding for Natural Monopolies—in General and with Respect to CATV," 7 *Bell Journal of Economics* 73 (1976).

Wilson, Carol, and Richard Karpinski, "Telcos Press Vendors for Video Solutions—Now," *Telephony*, April 26, 1993, at 8.

Wilson, Carol, "Bellcore Revisits the Residential Broadband Cost Question," *Telephony*, July 26, 1993, at 9.

Wireless Cable Association International, Comments, MM Docket No. 93-106 (June 14, 1993).

Case and Regulatory Proceeding Index

Name Index

Subject Index